The Dirty
Road
To Destiny

ISBN:0989826406
ISBN-13: **978-0989826402**

DEDICATION

This book is dedicated to the dreamers. I have always championed the hope of the human heart and I love the NO GIVE UP spirit in people. I am your cheerleader and I pray that no matter where you are now in life or where you have been will EVER detour you from your DESTINED PLACE in GOD!

CONTENTS

Acknowledgments

This book is a journey of the heart; it tells the story of the places that I have been, the people I have encountered along the way, and my evolutionary relationship with my God. It is a pilgrimage of passion; it is the relentless search for my Savior and the destiny that He has for me.

I want to thank my husband, Christopher J. Watts, for his love and encouragement. We are a "Team of Creative Memory Makers," baby, and we will leave an impression behind! I thank God for my beautiful, energetic girls, Antoinette, Analiese and Alexia; these three have taught me more than I anticipated learning!

I also want to acknowledge my mother. Without you there is no me, you are a rock, a strong tower, a hiding place, and your reflection looks so much like Jesus I can barely tell you two apart. I love you!

I learned so many practical life principles from my father, Isaiah Jackson, Sr. I miss you and love you, in glory we will meet again.

To the Kingdom Agenda International Ministry team, you guys are the real deal and I am honored to be a part of such an awesome ministry. Thank you, Pastor Andrews for helping me see God's potential inside me.

To my numerous family members and friends, each of you is a blessing and I am thankful to know you all, if I could name everyone, I would.

Without Christ, nothing in my life would make sense – Thank You can't touch the gratitude that I have for my Savior!!!

Introduction

I've always said that the most attractive people in the world are those who are comfortable just being who they are, with complete abandon. People with no pretenses, no excuses – just take it or leave it type people! Good or bad, it didn't matter, because you always know where you stand with them. I was determined to be that girl, just me, regardless of any extenuating circumstances.

At the time in my life when this story takes place, I knew, deep down, that I had to look in the mirror with my heart open and my eyes closed. I had so fixated on the outer self and afraid of what was inside me, that I avoided that moment for ten plus years.

But, eventually, I couldn't deny it was time for the two to meet. I had to face the reality of who I had become, the person I had allowed myself to be. I had to stop blaming people for the decisions that I had made. I had to own my life!

Accountability was hard for me. For many years, I had been running in circles, avoiding myself, and paralyzed with the fear of meeting that little girl. The two-year-old mesmerized by a television screen, losing herself in make believe, and merging fantasy with reality. I had created my own world and I would spend hours inside my own mind, imagining what that world would be like if only this or that would happen.

The day I faced that little girl who was trying so hard to impress the world, I emptied out my soul. I embraced who she was and all of who she still is: the innocence, the love, the selfishness, the loneliness, the hurt, and all the feelings of abandonment. I lived in her space for as long as I could; remembered her pain; remembered her joy. I looked into her spirit and saw forever. I had been pretending that I was someone else for so long that I convinced myself that who I had become wasn't a reflection of who she was. I had convinced myself that an all-knowing, ever-present God controlled my future, and because I had no real control over my life, I couldn't be held responsible for my own actions. I finally had to face the fact that I was responsible for the things I had allowed into my life. I had to acknowledge that the people that I allowed into my body and spirit, the words that spewed from my mouth, the lies I told, the deceptions I made, all belonged to me.

I loved that little girl in that place; she was so fresh and new, so willing to take on the world. I embraced her, and then I took all that was good and all that I believed to be bad, and laid it at the foot of the cross. Then I simply moved forward; after all what else was there to do.

This book is a result of that purge.

Maybe God was speaking and I was just not hearing Him beyond the distractions of the sea of other voices that roared like great tsunami waves in my mind. At this point in my life I just needed God to be tangible, someone I could reach out and touch, see or hear; I just wanted more. I didn't know what more meant or even what it was or how it would come about for that matter but I knew I had to take some drastic measures to behold God in all that He is. I knew that I would have to fight to see the Shekinah glory (open showing) of the Lord in my life.

I was a people pleaser. I have always wanted everyone to be okay with everything that I did or said. I wanted to be right or acceptable, no matter what.

I have tried my very best to live an expected life! What I mean by that is, an expectation by my definition is the belief of a predicted end. A pregnant woman expects to have a baby, a person who works a full week expects a full week of pay, and if you throw something up in the air, you expect it to come down, right? These are things that you believe will turn out the way you expect. The problem with expectation is, when the situation is not that black and white, everyone has his or her own belief of what the end will be, even if that end belongs to someone else.

I based many of my life altering decisions on the hopes

and beliefs that others had for me. I've often wondered what I would have done with my life, if I had listened to my own heart from the beginning instead doing what friends, family, and even society expected of me. After high school, you are expected to go to college. As a woman, you are expected to be a wife and a mother; you're expected to cook, clean, and cater to your man. As a black woman, I felt as though it was expected of me to be sassy, tough, and in control. As a daughter, I felt that it was expected of me to be perfect.

It can be hard to live up to the expectations placed upon you by others. Sometimes it is difficult to pretend to be someone that you are not, but so often we try to live up to an impossibility that we were never created to be. In the process we lose a part of ourselves, the true authentic self that God ordained and predestined for us to be.

Being " yourself " around another person is a luxury many take for granted. It seems to be such a simple task—*to just be*— but it was one of the hardest things for me to accomplish. To speak freely or voice a heartfelt opinion without worry or fear of being criticized is hard sometimes.

I have searched for that balance for a while now, wanting to glorify God in all of my ways without compromising my personality. Losing myself isn't the problem. I've learned that in order for me to exemplify Christ I must allow Alicia to die, but not that zeal for life, laughter, and peace; the perky way I dance; or the solemn way I examine my surroundings before I speak. Those things are a part of the gift God made when He created me and now I am faced with the beautiful task of how to show the world what is uniquely me, without shame or regret, while at the same time allowing the character of Christ to shine.

I have accepted that I cannot second-guess the voice of God. I can't depend upon second opinions from other people about whether to trust my instincts. I no longer have to worry or over analyze about confronting issues because of my concern of offending someone. I have learned Gods way. I need to live, to hope, to dream, to laugh, to trust, to reach, to dance, to write, to talk, to meditate, and to sing no matter who might tell me to stop. I've learned to trust the inner voice that whispers to my spirit and sometimes screams within me to move forward and just do *me*!

I'm not some renegade Christian; I don't believe that I can just do whatever I want without Godly counsel, but I am saying that I don't trust just *anybody* to speak into my life! I believe in accountability partners, set leaders, pastors, overseers, friends and loved ones, but beyond *all* of those trusted advisors, I trust Holy Spirit the *most*! God's word says that, at the time of salvation, I was sealed with the precious promise of Holy Spirit, and that He will be my guide on this journey called Life. He will lead and guide me into *all* truth for my life. He will convict me of my sins. Although I truly believe that most people are sincere when they point out your errors, I must say it is so not necessary to do.

I have spent countless hours, days, I can dare even say years trying to figure me out. I didn't want to wear the badges or labels that others had assigned to me. I was God's child and only He could stamp me, only he could define who I was and why I did what I did. So, in order for me to figure out me I had to know the mind of the creator. And now as I look back over my life I can pinpoint key events, specific words, particular people, and situations that God orchestrated to shape my way of thinking, doing and interacting.

It all started when I was a little girl, my earliest memory, believe it or not, was at two years of age. I was an unsocial and awkward child. I never really got along with or fit in with the crowd. I didn't like to play with other kids. I spent a lot of my time watching TV shows or reading books. I was happiest doing those things, but that behavior wasn't really fostered in the environment I grew up in. Children were supposed to be active, outside playing games, building things, and exploring the world. Television and books mesmerized me; I truly believe I had watched every show ever created at the time and flipped through more picture books than normal for my age. There is where I began to merge the fantasy of television with the reality of everyday life; in that place is where my faith foundation was laid. It was the place where I learned to dream.

I remember when I was about eight years old; I had gotten a tape recorder from my mom and pretended to be Oprah Winfrey. I gave myself an interview, asking the questions and giving the answers, typical childhood stuff, but the difference with me is that in my heart I knew I would be that person one day sitting on the couch like Oprah, chatting about my life! I was a dreamer, a visionary, and a big thinker from the beginning of my life and I expected a great end!

Warning

I make no apologies for my journey to my destined place in Christ, but I must warn you that the contents of this book are graphic at times. I was tempted to remove much of the graphic content so nobody would feel uncomfortable or question the validity of my walk with God, but I could not! I had to be as transparent as possible so that others could see where I was and how far I've come. My hope is that others who have had similar experiences can find the same freedom that I have found in Him.

I have learned so many life lessons from my mistakes, my bad behavior, and my disobedience. To be quite honest, I enjoyed my sin. I experienced a lot of pleasure and it was difficult to separate myself from it, but I did.

I have declared Proverbs 3: 5-6 over my life for as long as I can remember,

"Trust in the Lord with all thine heart; and lean not unto thine own

understanding. In all thy ways acknowledge him, and he shall direct thy paths."

I can't say that I always understood why I took the path that I did, but I can say that in good and bad, obedience and disobedience, I trusted God to make it all work out in the end!

This is my journey and if you are ready, I invite you to come along for the ride!

HOW IS IT POSSIBLE TO FEEL EVERYTHING AND NOTHING AT THE SAME TIME? IT WAS THE HARDEST THING FOR ME TO EXPLAIN, I HAD REACHED A POINT IN MY LIFE WHERE NOTHING MADE SENSE AND EVERYTHING WAS GOING WRONG. I HAD NO GRASP OF ANY SITUATION, CHAOS WAS AT MY DOORSTEP AND I STOOD READY TO OPEN IT. I'VE SAID NEVER.... TIME AND TIME AGAIN AND, MORE OFTEN THAN NOT, I'VE DONE NOTHING MORE THAN PROVE MYSELF TO BE A LIAR. THERE'S GOOD AND BAD IN US ALL AND WE ALL TEND TO HAVE OUR OWN IDEAS OF WHAT RESPECT, TRUTH, RIGHT & WRONG ARE. BUT BY WHOSE STANDARD DO YOU LIVE. NO ONE REALLY KNOWS WHAT ACTION THEY WILL TAKE UNTIL THEY'RE FACED WITH THE OPPORTUNITY TO DO JUST THAT, ACT (ASSERT CERTAIN THEOLOGIES). THIS IS MY STORY, WITHOUT THE SWEET AROMA OF APOLOGIES OR EXCUSES. IT IS WHAT IT IS. LIFE, MY PERCEPTION OF LIFE!

-ALIWATTS

CHAPTER 1
THE BECKONING

The wind gently breezed over my sweat-drenched body, bringing only momentary relief from the sweltering heat. It was an unusually warm day for early spring in southern California, but that didn't seem to bother me, I was somewhere else, somewhere in the deep recesses of my mind. My strides were determined; they frantically searched for release. I pushed my way through mile after mile, fighting for peace of mind and spirit, still searching for answers to the questions that I'd asked of myself for far too long now.

There was a perfect view in my path. The treadmill in the plush apartment complex gym, where I lived, was facing the pool;

which was surrounded by palm trees, waterfalls, and gazebos, but I looked beyond it not seeing, not hearing, or feeling a thing. I usually came here to shed the stresses of the day, I came here to forget and it didn't hurt that it kept my body tight and youthful, but today was different, today the memories flooded, the rivers ran deep and forgetting…. was not an option! I had been running away from the pain of decisions I had made years before, barely realizing even where I was or how I had gotten here. I loved the beauty of Southern California, but my heart, my past, my mistakes and I believe my future was still in Florida. I couldn't continue to run away from the guilt that I felt, I couldn't keep running away from the lies that I was living – I had to face them I had to face me!

I am and have always been a particularly private person, so any information that came out of me was very pointed and served its' purpose, but never revealed more than I wanted you to know. There's only one person in this world that I shared my heart with, and even she doesn't know the full story. So, for the demons that were hidden within I had to deal with alone and I knew that I would have a true fight on my hands.

I was the obligatory "good girl" to the naked eye. I didn't drink, smoke, or consistently hang out in the clubs. I had a very shy demeanor (so people said), but it wasn't me, not the real me, the person no one knew, the person I was afraid that no one would accept. The reality of the matter is that I had a mean streak, I was very opinionated; I had a wild side to me that was yearning to get out. I had ideas and dreams that were by most people's standards outlandish at best. And for what seemed like a lifetime I had repressed them. I didn't think like most people I hung around. I always felt different, but never felt comfortable enough to just be myself. So, I hid her, somewhere deep within, so deep, that I almost forgot about her, but not for long, because she would resurface one day to reconcile herself. I could no longer ignore that day.

"Hellooooo."

"Yeah, what's up?" I surprisingly answered as I snapped back to reality removing my headphones.

"Are you going to be on there much longer?"

I glance up at the clock and realize that I had lost track of time, I can't believe I've been on this treadmill for two hours. I slow my pace then attempt to step off the still moving walkway and lose my balance, but I catch myself and quickly sit on an exercise bike.

"Are you all right?"

"Yeah, I'm O.K., I just need to catch my breath, I think I might have over did it today. I just need a minute."

"You don't look so hot, let me get you some water."

"Thank you..."

"Jeff, Jeff Howard."

Jeff then hurriedly retrieves a bottle of water from his gym bag.

"Thanks, Jeff Howard, that was really sweet of you, do you always make it habit of saving ladies in distress?"

"Only the one's falling all over themselves."

"That's cute, real cute. Thanks again for the water and I guess I'll see you around." I say invitingly.

" I hope so."

Look at me flirting, will I ever learn. It's definitely not typical of me to hit on men, but Jeff sparked something in me. Maybe it was his chivalry; I was not used to men coming to my rescue. My mother always told me that I did too much to gain the attention or rather to keep the attention of men, but today the walls were coming down and I felt a shifting taking place on the inside of me, like an earthquake I could neither stop nor contain. I wonder where all that came from anyway. I hadn't thought about my past in years and now isn't the time to start bringing all that up. I had enough to deal with in my crazy relationship with Keilan.

When I finally get back to my apartment, I down about a gallon of water, I was seriously dehydrated. I take out some chicken for dinner and open a package of strawberries that I had been saving for a shortcake I promised my neighbor I would make for him, but he was out of town and it was all I had to snack on. When I walk into my bedroom, I stumble over a box of books that I had placed there the night before that I had obviously forgotten about. I pick the box up to move it out of the way and a picture falls from the bottom of it, I guess, it had been stuck there for a while. I pick it up and it's the old church gang, Gary, Angie, Rochelle, Chris, Taylor, Lois and Jason, I wonder what happened to all of them, I mean, I know where Gary is, but I haven't even thought about any of those guys before today, in years.

I shrug it off and run myself a hot bath, my skin is nice; I can't believe that I've never had a pimple. My sister was the exact opposite, she use to break out all the time, thank God I've never had to worry about that. I pour in some bubbles; turn on the radio and climb into the tub; I'm exhausted. "Sit back and relax, grab something or someone special and let me take you on ride. It's

Rockwell on the mic, bringing you the soulful sounds of Maxwell, Sade, Babyface and a whole lot more." His voice was soothing, but I couldn't help but to think that he was probably a Big Fat white man on the other end. Radio voices make you dream and fantasize of perfection in a man, somehow hoping the sexiness in his voice matched the mind, body and soul. That's why I never wanted to meet my favorite radio DJ's; I wanted to reserve my private moments alone in my room with my fantasies. I'm more than tired when I get into the tub, so I lie back into my tub and with lightning speed fall into a deep sleep. The memories came flooding back and transported me to a place I could no longer hide from.

CHAPTER 2
THE MAKING

Alicia Andrews, that's me, daughter of Anthony and Gwendolyn, born February 1974, in Panama City, Florida. I was different from the beginning of my life, an energetic, inquisitive, yet solemn little girl. I was type cast as the odd ball, because I tended to do things my way. I was known to sit underneath the kitchen table on beautiful sunny afternoons reading the latest Dr. Seuss book (my favorite was *Green Eggs and Ham)*, while the other kids in the neighborhood were out playing softball, building club houses, and playing Hide-and-Go-Seek. I played with them sometimes but mostly I kept to myself. I was the third and final child that my parents would have together. My older brother was less than two years older than me and my sister was less than one year my senior. Needless to say, we managed to keep our parents busy.

My mother never mentioned or spoke ill of my father and he chose, for his own reasons, not to be there to watch me grow, to teach me, or to love me. He, like far too many of our men, just walked away without explanation, without reason, seemingly, without care.

By the time I was two, my parents had made the decision to divorce and my mother had moved on and remarried. I didn't find out until much later what really happened with them, I guess knowing the truth made it easier for me to forgive my dad for his absence, but it never could excuse him for not checking in or supporting us. I believe that men, who walk away, no matter the circumstance, are cowards, plain and simple. Can they redeem themselves? I believe it's possible, but it's *not* easy!

I had so many questions about life that were unanswered. I know now that I never received any answer because I never asked the questions to anyone other than myself. I didn't have the answer; that was already apparent, and it didn't occur to me at the time to address God because I, at that time in my life, wasn't taught to speak to Him, pray to Him or seek Him for specific answers to real life situations. I was raised on clichés and anecdotes like "God will make a way" and "Jesus is the answer for the world today." But, I never really knew what any of that meant. Because I didn't understand God, the decisions I made in my life would take me down paths that could have been avoided, if only I had established a relationship. Instead, I tried to fulfill an obligation to the people around me, who believed that as long as you were in church you were o.k.

I don't despise my upbringing. I was born into a large, loving family, but when it came to God, I feel as though many of my family members were misguided and only did what they saw others before them do. They never searched for more beyond tradition.

God had a plan for my life that required knowledge of Him.

He had a desire to establish a relationship with me, as He does with all of His creation. Although I can't say that I understand the circumstances that led me to Christ, I do know I am eternally grateful that when my father and mother were faced with the tough decision to trust God and His Word or to trust man and his word, they chose God.

I wish I could say I had a picture-perfect family life, but like many of you, I would be lying if I tried to convince you that all was well with me as a child. I don't remember ever living with my biological father, although at some point I know that I did. My first recollection of meeting my father was in my mid teens, at my uncle and aunt's home. He was sitting in a chair in their living room, leaned back with his feet stretched out in front of him, crossed at the ankle. He was and still is a tall, dark-skinned, thin man with very distinguished features, a handsome man by most standards. It was the 80's and back then large, gold hoop earrings were the style to be wearing and being like most typical teenagers I had me a pair on. It was a typical day, I was hanging out with my cousins doing giggly, girlfriend-type things, laughing, gossiping, writing notes, and searching for a snack every few minutes; I paid no attention to the stranger sitting in the corner. It soon became obvious that he knew me, because he immediately started chastising the size of my earrings.

"Take those earrings out of your ears, what do you think you're grown now?" he declared.

I was confused, because I had no idea who this guy was. My aunt saw the confusion on my face.

"Girl, you don't know who this is, do you?" she said.

"No ma'am." I answered.

And that's my first valid memory of my father. Nice huh.

I never considered him my Dad, nor did I care what he thought about my earrings. My mother had married the man that I would call Dad years before. He was the man who raised me, helped put a roof over my head, and allowed his life to be the instrument that led me to God. He helped my family establish a much needed relationship with the Trinity. It was not an easy road traveled. I even feel some trepidation attempting to recall the journey, because it is filled with bittersweet memories. I don't feel comfortable blaming or pointing out the flaws of others because it highlights the negative and sometimes overshadows all the good and positive attributes that a person brings to the table, so I will choose my words carefully.

I loved my dad dearly and am disappointed in myself that while he was yet living I didn't verbalize it as much as I wanted to. He called me his baby girl and I know that he loved me to death. Over the years, I have learned much about love and how people express the emotion we call love. Love is an emotion we choose to utilize; it is not something we fall into. Unlike what most of us think about love, we can help who we love, it is a conscience decision we make. I have also learned a thing or two about pain and how pain translates into action; "Hurting people, hurt people!" Before my father established a personal relationship with Christ, his anger got the best of him more often than I should have witnessed. As a child, I didn't understand how, in one moment he could be so loving and nurturing, and in the next loose it. I watched my mother balance protecting their love, shielding him from the hurt; showing us what real love looked like. She might not have known it then, but she showed us what forgiveness looked like; she showed us 1 Corinthians 13. She exemplified the character of God, even when life just wasn't fair to her. I first heard this saying from a former pastor of mine, and what it means is that when a person is hurt their natural reaction is to transfer their negative feelings into something or on to someone, in order to attempt to make themselves feel better.

When I understood the dynamic of these two emotions, it made the turbulent relationship between my mom and dad, even my biological father make more sense to me and it helped me shift my pain in a more positive direction. Not overnight, mind you, but when I take the time to put things into perspective I am able to process my feelings more clearly.

My dad eventually got a handle on his anger issues after he surrendered his life to Christ and to be quite honest, most of our lives together were quite happy. He was an excellent provider and he loved my mother so deeply. He raised us as if we were his biological children, never once heard him refer to us as his stepchildren, NEVER. I can still hear his laughter in my mind; he truly was a great man.

Our household was relatively "normal" for the most part, where family was very important. My mother was the most loving, kind, considerate, and giving person that I have ever known. When I was six she gave birth to my youngest brother, her fourth child of whom I was insanely jealous. She also helped raise her younger brother after my grandmother was disabled due to stroke. We were a close-knit family, a God fearing family, who loved one another at all times, even if sometimes it didn't always feel like it.

My mother never complained, she took care of us all, worked a full time job and always seemed happy. Whatever problems she may have had being a mother to us was never evident to me, she was and still is my personification of perfection in a woman. God was in her eyes, in her smile, in her touch, and in her voice. My stepfather likewise worked long hours and was rarely home and my oldest brother had this crazy notion that he had the right to discipline me while my parents were out working and my sister somehow seemed to believe the same. They were always telling me what to do and what I could or could not say. Even before my mom remarried, they usurped a roll they were never asked to fill. I didn't remember my father and it never bothered me that he was gone, but it never occurred to me that maybe they did remember and they were only doing what they had been in a since forced to do, be the man and woman of the house in my parents absence.

I lost my voice during that time, because I never had the

opportunity to speak it, not literally mind you, but for some reason I began to retreat within myself, because every time I had something to say, I was always being told to be quiet or shut up by somebody. We all couldn't be the boss and to be honest with you I didn't want the job. I quickly became an observer of my surroundings rather than a doer in them, as a defense. When I did choose to speak, I was often critical, which was interpreted as me being mean. So, silence and solitude became my comfort; it was what made me feel safe. But, that too was taken the wrong way and soon I was seen as stuck up or antisocial. I never felt comfortable in my own skin. I never felt like I fit anywhere, or belonged to anyone. I loved my family, but there was something very different about me. I was the 'ugly duckling' and boy, did I know it.

I guess, in some ways, they were right. I was a weird little kid. In grade school, the only friends I had were family; all my playmates were cousins or siblings. I never attempted to make new or different friends. I didn't want to. Besides, the ones I had got on my nerves. I couldn't get rid of them; they were family. You can't choose when it comes to family; they come with the package.

When I was fifteen, I met my first boyfriend, Calvin Jenkins; we all called him, CJ. He was the best friend of my cousin's boyfriend. You know how it goes when you're that age. Your sister, friend, or cousin (in this case), has a boyfriend and the only way that she can get out of the house is to say she's going somewhere with you, because you were the "good one." I was the one all the parents trusted. It was a tall order to fill, a responsibility I didn't want, but I was forced to take for the sake of everyone else's freedom.

I went out a lot then, because like I said, I was the scapegoat for all my female relatives, but I never liked any of the guys who tagged along for the ride. CJ was different; he was nice, respectful, and almost shy. I saw a bit of myself in CJ. He was soft spoken, a person of few words, but through his eyes I could see his heart and it had more than enough room for me to rest in. I was young and knew nothing of emotional love, familial love yes, but for a stranger, I had no idea, but I was willing to learn whatever it was he was obviously willing to teach.

He spoiled me with flowers, candy, teddy bears, and jewelry. I use to think that he was a drug dealer, but he swore to me that he wasn't. His mom was an addict, and because of that, he assured me, he would never sell. I wanted to believe him. CJ worked two jobs, was in school, and played football, so I couldn't see where he would have the time. Yet, he always had an abundance of cash that most teenagers just shouldn't have. Still, I chose to trust him.

I trusted him with everything, I was so comfortable around him because I could speak and be myself without criticism. He liked me for who I was, there were no pretenses with him and I felt comfortable just being *me*.

✝✝✝

I don't remember much about, on campus, high school life. The four years that I attended are vague to me. I remember the prom, a few school dances, homecoming, marching band (yes, I was a geek), and oh, one talent show in particular, but that's really it.

It was the eighties, the time of Kid & Play, En Vogue, poky dots, big hair, break dancing & African symbols. We were all like walking robots, mimicking everything that we saw, our hairstyles, our clothes, the way we talked, walked and danced.

There were these two guys Barry and Derrick, who just knew they were Kid & Play, we even called them that. They styled there hair like them, dressed like them and danced like them, it may sound corny now, but then they were cool, all the girls were smitten, even me.

It took a lot to be yourself back then and 99% of us didn't

have the courage to follow the beat of our own hearts, there was too much pressure to be like someone else, you either followed the crowd willingly, got drug in by association (family) or you were ostracized for being "unique."

Unique, such a pretty word, unlike weird, strange, nerdy, goofy, stupid, four eyes, and the plethora of off the wall comments a cruel teenager, trying to fit in, could hurl in the direction of a brave soldier marching to the beat of his own drum. Somehow they managed to make it through each day, some bewildered and beat down and some seemingly unaffected. I wish I was that brave or strong at that point in my life, but I wasn't. I bordered between the two groups, the in and the out crowd, I dressed the part and even hung out in the 'right' people, but I was a silent unwilling participant, wishing that I had the courage to march to the music within.

The day I knew there was power in being unique is settled in my mind like a cat in a warm basket of clothes straight from the dryer. It was the day of the student talent show. You had to buy tickets to attend the talent show, because it was during class time. If you really wanted to get out of class, they literally made you pay. There were two separate shows at the end of the day, and if you were smart, you bought a ticket for each show, went to one, and ditched for the rest of the day on the other. I went to the first show and just like we all expected, Barry and Derrick rocked the house with a jazzy rendition of dance moves straight from the videos of Kid 'n Play. But that wasn't the highlight for me.

Gary Froman was one of the brave and few, a quiet guy that everyone knew of because he was definitely different, but no one really knew on a personal level, he wasn't in style, he wore what he chose and seemed unconcerned with the world around him. When they announced him, there was an immediate hush over the audience, and believe me, that was a challenge in a room of rowdy teenagers. My mind raced with the possibilities of what he was about to perform; he was so quiet and reserved that I was at the edge of my seat waiting to see what in the world Gary was going to do.

The curtain opened to Gary standing behind a turntable. He began to sing a song, which he'd explained beforehand, that he had written himself. He had a heavenly voice. Then, out of nowhere, the music kicked in and the crowd went wild. It was a familiar sound, hype; yet clean, (I know that doesn't make sense, but the sound was somehow more pure than the music we normally listened to). Gary was charismatic and the crowd responded with thunderous electricity. We didn't truly know why, but Gary did.

Offstage, people responded to Gary much differently than they did that night. They often talked bad about him behind his back, and some were even mean enough to do it to his face. He wasn't the snazziest dresser; he wore thick black-rimmed glasses, had a few extra shades of black on him, and didn't talk much to other people. None of this ever seemed to bother Gary — or at least that's the way I saw it. He was content to be himself and that day, at the talent show, I saw the benefits of just being you.

Just a few minutes before Gary went on I saw him standing at the

bottom of the stairs preparing to go on, Jason Bellflower (the

biggest jerk on earth), said something to Gary that caused him to

bend over and when he did, Jason pushed him to the ground.

Gary sat there for a second and waited for Jason to leave. I could

see that Gary was noticeably shaken, but unlike most of us, who

no matter what the circumstance, would have at least in the

shock of the situation, lashed back by instinct alone, but not Gary.

Jason walked away laughing, seemingly proud of what he had just

done, then Gary got up brushed himself off and walked onto the

stage as if nothing had happened. I didn't understand at the time

why that moment was so important I just knew that it was.

I wanted to personally congratulate Gary on the

impressive job he did up there, but just before I could head in his

direction, the bell rang and the crowd scattered. I had only a few

minutes to get off campus before the second talent show started

and the head count began, so I chose to forget about it. I quickly gathered my books and rushed to the front gate where CJ would be waiting for me.

I was beaming with the confidence to finally just be myself, follow my own heart, dress the way I wanted, style my hair the way I thought proper, just be me— but the second I laid my eyes on CJ, I lost it. What would he think of me? What would he say? I was too afraid of the answers to those questions, so I eliminated the opportunity of them ever being brought up.

CJ had this grey Monte Carlo that looked like he had spray painted it, but it got us to where we were going and that's all that I cared about; it was my chariot. We had been planning this day for weeks; I trusted CJ with everything, my heart, my mind, and now my body would be his as well. CJ and his friends had a special clubhouse they built in his back yard. This was not your normal clubhouse, it had a couch, a bed, dining table and a TV inside; those guys were imaginative to say the least. They had to make reservations with one another to use it, and today was ours to share, alone, at "The Clubhouse."

I experienced a lot of firsts with CJ, my first slow dance, my first flowers, my first kiss, my first lover, my first love, and, of course, my first heartache. I often wish that he wasn't the one who had to break me in. We were good together, but we were young and impetuous, and we believed in a love we didn't quite understand at the time.

<u>When you're young, love is new and beautiful and that's the way you expect it to stay. Yet, when it changes, unfortunately, so do you.</u>

At that age, you think it's cool that your parents aren't super strict. I could come and go pretty much as I pleased. Don't get me wrong, I did have rules, but I didn't feel smothered. Do I wish I had been guarded more? Honestly, now I can say yes, it allowed me to walk through doors that I never should have known existed. But, at the time, I enjoyed the freedom.

✞✞✞

He had never mentioned her before the day she showed

up on his doorstep. I had always assumed that I was his first, just like he was mine. After all, he was only seventeen; you're not supposed to have a past at seventeen, but he did.

Mary Frances.

What type of name is that for a black girl from a little country town? They dated before we met, he tried to explain, but I wasn't paying him any mind. I didn't want him to see her; she had to go.

She was in town, visiting some relatives, and wanted to spend some time with him before she went back home to Tallahassee. I couldn't even believe that he would consider it; this girl wasn't even cute. And what about me? He shouldn't even want to see her; he had me now. She was in his past, and as far as I was concerned that's where she needed to stay. After a few tantrums and some crocodile tears from me, he agreed not to see her. Maybe a little too quickly, now that I think about it.

The night I found out Mary Frances was in town; my

girlfriends and I decided to go to the big local high school football game. I needed to get out after the drama with CJ earlier that day. I had a feeling that something crazy was going to happen, but I still went. Our school was playing our rivals from across town, so excitement was in the air. My girls and I planned to go to the local teen hangout after the game, to keep my mind off my situation with CJ.

We got to the game late, and of course, spent all our time walking around the stadium, trying to be cute. But, my girl Stephanie wasn't thinking about being cute, she was looking for trouble, as usual. Stephanie was notorious for dating guys who treated her like crap, and she had a knack for putting us into the middle of her drama.

That night, the subject of her mayhem was Denise Carter; her so-called-man's other girl. But, if truth was told, Denise was his girl; Stephanie was the chick on the side. But, you couldn't tell her that. Stephanie was bold as all get out, but Denise didn't play games when it came to her man. She would fight at the drop of a dime. The word on the street was that Denise was planning to beat up Stephanie that night, for moving in on her territory. We all knew that if those two crossed paths, some stuff was going down. Everyone was on the lookout, trying to prevent the ensuing mess.

I was in line at the snack bar, and Candy had gone to the restroom, while Jackie and Cassandra were talking to some classmates on the other side of the field. I was stuck babysitting Stephanie and her escalating temper, but we were standing just a few feet from the concession stand and Candy would be back in just a second. Stephanie promised she would be good; why did I walk away? What made me think she would behave?

As I stood in line, I noticed Stephanie taking off her earrings. Before I could respond, she had punched Denise in the back of the head. She couldn't have picked a worse time to act a fool. Arms and hair were flying all over the place. By the time we got there, Denise had pulled her knife out and cut Steph on her back. Security broke up the fight before things got out of hand. Tensions were still running high; both girls were still frustrated, so we took the brigade down the street to Willie's, the local teen club.

When we got there, Denise is nowhere to be found and Steph was hot. The knife had barely broken her skin, but that was the least of our concerns. Because they acted up at a school-sponsored function, we were all candidates for expulsion. I've never seen my cousin Candy more mad, because she was our class valedictorian. If Stephanie had ruined that for her, she didn't have to worry about Denise, because Candy was going to whoop her behind. Everybody was freaking out and it took some serious persuasion too calm them down, but I managed to do just that.

After thirty minutes, the whole situation was all but forgotten. We were headed into the club when who do I see walking across the parking lot without a care in the world, none other than my sweetheart, CJ.

I never thought he'd have the nerve to bring that girl up there as if I wasn't going to show up; he knew my plans for the night. I guess his timing was off, seeing as how we got kicked out of the game at half time. He promised me that he wouldn't see her, but there they were walking side-by-side. She was gazing at him like he was a chocolate covered Snickers bar and she needed satisfying. I felt my blood boiling in my veins, something I had never felt before. I almost lost control, but I managed to pull myself back, after all the convincing I had just done to get Candy and Stephanie to come to their senses.

I was going to handle it later, you know, be civilized and ask him about it later. I would give him an opportunity to be honest or to dig his own grave; it was all up to him.

"Ain't that CJ walking with some girl over there?" Stephanie seemed to yell. Why did she have to see that? Now I have to act foolish. "I know you're not going to let him punk you out like that, you better check him. Don't worry we got your back girl."

I was practically forced to do the unthinkable and like a swarm of bees to a hive, we moved in. He could feel us coming and as he turned his head to look over his shoulder, I clock him in the side of the face with a furious, open-palm smack. I could see the shock and fear in his eyes when he realized that it was me. You'd better believe that I was just as shocked and scared as he was. I wasn't the type to get all belligerent and ghetto, but I was so pissed, hurt, and embarrassed that I couldn't help myself.

He couldn't say anything, and to be honest I wouldn't have heard him anyway. I had checked out. I was still standing there, but part of me was gone; the part that cared to have an explanation of his actions just disappeared. I no longer had any expectations of him or anyone else. That night I changed; I took a turn on my destined path. I wasn't sure if the change was good or bad, but I knew things were different than they'd been five minutes before.

Suddenly, someone starts to run, which snaps me out of

my state of insanity. Collectively, we made a mad dash towards

the car and jumped in. Stephanie tried to crank it up, but the car

stalled and Denise was standing right in front of us. It didn't take a

rocket scientist to realize that she was still mad. We all used to

clown on "The Duce;" that's what we called Steph's car. It would

always stop in the middle of traffic, wouldn't crank, or would run

out of gas because her gages didn't work, but tonight that mess

wasn't funny. There was Denise with her feet planted and a gun

pointed square in the middle of Stephanie's forehead, and The

Duce was playing games. Steph was a champ though; she didn't

panic. She just pumped that pedal like she was mining oil,

slammed her foot on the gas, and sped, full-throttle, towards

Denise. The car actually hit the girl. Well, more like knocked her

off balance. She was far enough away to react as the car came

toward her. I even think she got a round off before she fell to the

ground. We didn't really hurt her; we just had to get her out of

the way.

We laughed all the way home. Man, that was one night I

will, for many reasons, never forget.

CJ was apologetic after the club incident, but I couldn't forgive him. I didn't blame him for any of it and I never asked for an explanation. He had hurt me, made me feel things that I never wanted to feel. It changed me. It changed love for me.

I stayed for a little while after it all, trying to make things work, I guess. But it wasn't the same. I left him after three years together. I still wanted to be with him, but I was too stubborn to give him another chance.

When I decided to leave CJ there was a lot going on in my life, both emotionally and spiritually. He took me on a roller coaster ride of emotions. I hit every peak and wallowed in every valley. Even as I walked away, I wanted him to hold me, to kiss me and tell me that everything was going to be all right, yet at the same time I was cursing his very existence. A mild case of schizophrenia was the best way to describe my mood. I was indecisive, manic, a flat out witch! The truth is, I was just a little girl trying to deal with grown-woman issues.

CHAPTER 3
THE DECISION

Every Sunday we would religiously make the trip to church, blind to the principles that were being ingrained into our psyche. I sat dutifully in the pew, listening to sermons that went in one ear and out the other. I was young and ignorance was bliss. I had no worries then; I had no guilt then; I didn't feel accountable for my actions *then*.

Around the time CJ and I were having our 'domestic' problems, my mother was asking my brother, sister, and I to go to this new church with her. I didn't want to go; I was comfortable where I was, and I couldn't understand what the big deal was about this new church. A church was a church, and God was God, no matter where you were, right? She was the one who forced us to go to the church we were already attending. But, after CJ and I split, I didn't care much about anything. So, when my mother asked one day, I couldn't muster up an excuse. I just went.

It was immediately evident that there was something very different about this new church. The people were all so happy and young. No one seemed to have a care in the world. They were friendly, almost to a fault. When the Pastor began his sermon, I was immediately puzzled. I knew that he was using the same Bible they used at my other church, because I had one in my hand. But, I had never heard much of it before and I definitely had never read it right along with the Pastor. It was as if he was speaking directly to me, and to me alone. My heart was beating so hard when he gave alter call; I just knew every person within ten miles could hear it. I felt like everything that I wanted in my life at that moment would be made whole, if I just got to my feet and walked to the alter for prayer. I wanted to receive the forgiving power of salvation through Jesus Christ; it was something I had never been offered before.

But, my feet were frozen; I was petrified of what people

would think of me. They would know that I had been having sex, cussing, and carrying on. I couldn't do it, even though I wanted to. The simple function of standing and walking, at that moment, was impossible to perform. I attended services for several weeks before I had the courage to listen to the voice coming from within, but I did do it eventually. At the age of eighteen, I gave my life to the Lord. In a way, I was hoping that the love that I felt like I had lost with CJ would be replaced, and for a time it was.

But, I also wanted to change; I didn't like the person I was becoming. I was mean and indifferent. I wanted so much to be like my mother. Everyone respected and loved her. I respected her and loved her more than anyone, so I chose to live my life by certain guidelines, imposed by the church and the Holy Bible. And I was happy with that decision, because it was one that I made on my own.

This new church gave me an extended family; my sisters and brothers in Christ seemed to calm the battle within me.

Attending a 'young' church (the eldest member was in their mid forties) made living a purified life that much easier for me, because I could see myself in them. Life was good and everything seemed right with the world. I was happy.

During that time, I was incredibly impressionable and wore my heart on my sleeve. I, without a doubt, inherited that from mom. I loved attending Wednesday night and Sunday morning service. It's where I went for peace of mind and the strength to resist the constant temptation of returning to a simpler life with no accountability, clubbing on the weekend, and sex as an option. The church was my refuge, my hiding place. I depended on it like I did food and water.

I soon made friends with some of the younger members in the church, and I ran into someone I already knew. The preacher's son was none other than Gary Froman. Turns out, Gary was the minister of music for the church. He composed and performed his own music; he was a Christian rap artist. Gary wasn't the strong silent type that everyone made him out to be in high school, he just spared his words for the right time and the right occasion. It all made sense now; at the talent show, Gary wasn't entertaining us, he was ministering to our souls.

✝✝✝

Out of all the people I would meet during that time in my life, nobody would be as close and as influential to me as Lois Bradley.

Lois and I both attended the local junior college where we, with the help of some other members of the church and fellow student body, formed an organization which fostered our belief that all men should be saved or at least know Christ as their personal savior.

Lois and I were close, maybe too close. She was my girl, the person outside of my family who I spent the most time with. Lois had two kids. Her oldest son lived in Wyoming with his grandmother, for reasons we never discussed. Some things are better left alone, you know?

Everyone has a story about why they choose to serve the Lord. Not all of us come through tragedy, but tragedy is one of the reasons that we do come. Lois was no exception.

She was married to a man who abused her both physically and mentally. She drank a lot, and smoked weed for recreation or maybe to numb the pain of her circumstances.

She trusted me with personal moments; things you sometimes have trouble admitting to yourself. She told me that one day her husband came home early and she didn't have the dinner prepared. It never took much to trigger him: not having the dinner ready or not anticipating his every move were enough to cause him to beat her like a rag doll. One day, he threw her down a flight of stairs, which knocked her unconscious. He left her there, with the children screaming and crying for her to get up. When she finally came around, she had the presence of mind to take her children, with nothing but the clothes on their backs, and leave. She told me that this wasn't the first time that he had did her this way, but that day was different, that day she had finally had enough.

She drove to Florida where her brother lived with his family, and where I lived with mine. She was safe from him there and could finally start over. Eventually, she started going to church. She learned that she was worth so much more than she had allowed herself to believe. She learned to love Lois all over again, the same way I learned to love and trust people around me again. It took some convincing and time, but eventually she gave up the alcohol and marijuana. Lois had been at the church for a while before I showed up, but it didn't take long for us to get to know one another. I respected her a great deal for the sacrifices she made so her children would have a better life. It was tough being a single mother, and I was more than happy to help her out; her son was a delight.

✟ ✟ ✟

Being saved was harder than I thought it would be. I had to give up a lot more than I had initially anticipated. I mean I knew pre-marital sex was off the list, but I had broken up with CJ, so that wasn't a problem anymore. What I never anticipated was giving up my music, going out with my friends, and cussing (the hardest challenge). There were so many rules. I'd expected to have to change some of my behavior, but this life was work. At my age, work was a bad word, yet I pressed on because I really did love God.

It's not like I cussed a lot anyway, but when I did it was automatic; you know, the word just fit with what I was trying to say. I wasn't being rude or disrespectful; I was just trying to get my point across where anyone listening would get it. In the semi-altered words of Lauryn Hill, "I add a motherjoka so you ignorant ni**as hear me." You know what I mean.

I made a conscious effort to make the necessary changes it

took to do right, but it didn't happen overnight. One day, I

realized that I hadn't cussed in a while, and sex didn't even enter

my mind. Through my example, some of my friends from high

school had joined the church, and I had made so many new ones.

Gary supplied the music, which sounded almost identical to the

music I was listening to before, but with a positive twist.

I read my Bible and I enjoyed it; I learned so much about

life thumbing through its pages. It wasn't a cakewalk, but what in

life worth anything, is? I figured if I could do it, anybody could.

The young adults in the church (ages 18-25) were an

eclectic bunch. We came from all walks of life, but, with the

exception of Gary, we all had one thing in common: we were all

babes in Christ. We had too much zeal and too little knowledge to

go out and conquer the world for the Kingdom. But with proper

guidance, we were able to venture out slowly to make a

difference. We would go to the juvenile detention center once a

month to talk to the kids and let them know that it was possible to do something positive with their lives. We were just like them, doing it in church. We would minister through song, dance, skits, poetry or just plain talking to them one-on-one, for real. I was always bluntly honest with them: I told them about my sexual past, my dirty mouth, and my fighting. I let them know what I replaced it with, that I was genuinely happy, and no one was twisting my arm to say or do anything.

Gary was brave enough to tell them that, at age nineteen, he was still a virgin and he was waiting until he was married before having sex. That was a big deal. They didn't always respond, but they got the opportunity to make a decision. They got a chance to see the other side of the coin and that always made me feel good. It made me feel useful, like I was contributing to the betterment of society, not just hoping and wishing for things to change.

I was so naïve as a young adult. Looking back now, I can truly say that I didn't know much; I was just free. Youth is a gift that is taken for granted. If I knew then what I know now, my choices would have been very different. But, I can't go back – you can't go back; so making the days count is imperative!

I placed a heavy burden on the friendships and relationships that I had established with people; that was a mistake! I expected that as I changed, everyone connected to me should change as well. The old church gang, we had some fun together, but we didn't all grow in God at the same pace and I was too new to this saved life to understand why people didn't just get it!

Angie was a pretty girl with beautiful, flawless skin, a perfectly shaped, voluptuous body, perfect teeth, and the brightest eyes you've ever seen. She dressed the part and said all the right things in the right places to the right people at the right time. She seemed perfect and I wanted what it is she appeared to have: a loving relationship with God and a true to desire to serve in the house of God.

We went to the same college, but for some odd reason I

didn't really see her much at school. Rumors of girls who flaunted themselves in front of the star athletes were common, and the atmosphere of freedom that a college campus fostered was a dangerous mix for testosterone filled males and young women unattended.

I began to hear her name whispered around campus as the go-to-girl for a good time. I didn't believe what I was hearing at all. At first I thought because it was such a big campus, there was bound to be more than one girl by the same name. Eventually, that was shot down as an option. Not all my friends were saved, they liked to be messy and gossip. They couldn't wait to tell me about the little church girl acting like a "street walker," as they would put it. One of my girlfriends from high school had to make a believer out of me! So, after class she said, "Get in the car with me and I will drive you over to the ball players' housing. You'll see her car parked there, just watch."

So, we went, and low and behold, there was Angie coming out of the ball players' apartment, all hugged up with a player, kissing and touching – I was shocked.

The following Sunday she showed up at church just as she always had, dressed properly, smiling beautifully, with a twinkle in her eye. She was the perfect little church girl in front of the right people, in the right place, at the right time, and I was offended! Why I took others actions so personally, I don't know. But I did, I just did. She was the first of many disappointments that I turned a blind eye to at the time, but gradually I allowed others' actions to chip away at the faith I had placed in the church and the people that attended such places.

If I had only known then, that I was suppose to be building a relationship between me and God, rather than building it upon my relationships with others; yes, I would have traveled some very different paths.

CHAPTER 4
CATALYST MOMENT

Lois was a little older than I was and, of course, with the children she had more responsibility. She had a nice three-bedroom apartment in a project development in the red eye district. It wasn't the greatest neighborhood, but it wasn't bad either. We spent most of our time together there, laughing and sharing life. The rest of our time was divided between church and class, so keeping secrets wasn't easy, not that it crossed my mind to keep secrets from Lois.

Because Lois was a single mother and living on her own, her place became the spot where all the single people would congregate for social activities: Bible study, watching movies, listening to music, and just talking. We were all young and very much human, so we still had issues with sexual curiosity, old friends, and old habits, but you never would know that by talking with or hanging out with us. The conversations that we had were always so 'holy' when we were all together; no one would ever admit that they were struggling in their daily life with God. Everybody seemed to be in full control of their every action or spoken word. I believed I was the only one having major issues, so I never said anything. I felt like I must be doing something wrong, so I just prayed about it and hoped that things would get easier.

Lois and I were more candid with one another when we were alone, and I confided in her when things got rough for me. She was always comforting, even if she had nothing to say. I laid my heart on the table when I walked into her home and never once did I think twice about its safety there.

I began to notice that Lois was accumulating quite a collection of nice, expensive items for the kids, herself, and the apartment. For a woman without a job or a man, this was strange.

None of us were rich by any means. We were comfortable for our age, but even I couldn't afford a lot of extras — with no rent, no bills, no children, and my parents and the government helping me with college.

Lois was a certifiable shopaholic, and had rather expensive taste, but I knew she couldn't afford her habit, so I questioned her. She justified buying it all with school grants, and child support, which made sense, so I dismissed it as nothing. But, soon there was something that I couldn't overlook.

Jason Briggs, a leader in the church and a brother in Christ, was more than friendly with Lois outside of church functions. He helped Lois with her son, he bought them gifts, and he took them on outings to the beach, movies, and amusement parks. I even tagged along a couple of times; he was a very nice man. It all seemed perfectly innocent, and would have been totally acceptable if it weren't for the fact that he had a wife and two children of his own. He rarely spent this type of time or attention on his family.

It bothered me that he would come by her place so often, but she assured me that nothing was going on between them. She said everything was on the up and up. She was my sister and he was my brother; all of us had been taught the same Word, from the same Bible, from the same ministers. I never believed they would lie to me, or anyone else for that matter.

Then, one Saturday night, I was working the late shift, as usual, when my boss decided to let me go a little early. I worked at the Kentucky Fried Chicken in town, but because it was Spring Break, everyone migrated to the beaches at night and business was slow.

I could feel that something was wrong. Getting off from work was no surprise, and it had nothing to do with this feeling I had; I just knew something was wrong. After leaving work, I decided to stop and see Lois, to catch up on the week. We had been playing phone tag for a few days; both of us had been too busy with school, work, and different church functions to keep up.

When I pulled up, I noticed Jason's car parked in front of her apartment. I was stunned at first, and then shocked, and finally, I was just angry. The same feeling that I had when I saw CJ with that girl was back; it was that feeling of being completely out of control.

I began to leave, but something wouldn't let me turn a blind eye, so I pulled back into the space and sat there for a minute to calm down.

It was a clear December night. The sky was so black it seemed colorful, so strong you could feel it. I couldn't move, couldn't think of why I was sitting there. I let my mind drift into nothingness, for what seemed like an eternity. If I had a lucid thought at all I don't remember it. I was numb. In that stretch of time, however long it was, something broke in me. Something changed in me on that clear December night, sitting in my car, without a lucid thought in my mind.

Maybe I was naive in thinking that because you went to

church that you practiced what was preached; I just assumed that most people were honest, like me. I had given up a lot, just like everybody else, so I had no problem making character judgments. Lois and I had countless sessions of candidness and complete abandon in her apartment. I'd given the secrets of my closet some air, but she'd been keeping big secrets locked away.

After regaining my composure, I decided to go in. I needed to see with my own eyes, what my heart was telling me. Too afraid to knock, I stood there with my head pressed against the hard, cold, metal frame. I was hoping to hear something to calm my nerves, but after standing there for what seemed like forever, without a sound, I mustered up the courage to knock. Immediately, I heard scrabbling about and whispers that I could barely make out. It infuriated me and hurt to know that they would jeopardize their families and subject their children to this kind of pain and embarrassment.

When Lois finally opened the door, Jason was nowhere to

be found, and she was pathetically thrown together and out of breath.

"Where's Brian?" I asked.

"Oh, he's spending the night with Liz and the boys," she said just as Jason walked out of the restroom.

"Thanks for letting me use your bathroom, I don't think that I would have made it home if I wouldn't have stopped," he said nervously.

They both rambled on with some ridiculous story that I never heard. I couldn't listen to them; one solitary thought kept running through my head,

Her son is at Liz's house (his wife), while she's here screwing her husband!

I could not, for the life of me, understand why she would keep such a secret from me. Maybe I wouldn't have reacted the way that I did if she had just told me.

After Jason excused himself to go home to his family, she tried to explain, but I wasn't receptive. I had lost my trust in people again, just that quick. The closer a person was to me, the deeper the hurt and the thicker the wall I built around me became.

For months, I tried to stay focused, but that night ran through my head like a broken record. I went to church, but I wasn't really there; I couldn't get Lois's betrayal out of my head. She was a worship leader and praise dancer, with the grace of a gazelle and he a minister. His wife was clueless about what was going on, or maybe she just didn't care. I couldn't receive anymore. I was suspicious of everybody in the church, and I didn't know whom to believe. Soon I began to question where I had placed my trust, in God or these people.

✝✝✝

I spent a lot of my time with my younger cousins after that, because the adults asked too many questions and I had no desire to answer them. The kids were innocent, they were free to do as they pleased, I felt comfortable around them, and I trusted them.

One afternoon I took the kids with me to the bookstore; I needed research material for a report and the children loved to play in the kids' corner. As I was walking through the aisles, Kay, my three-year-old cousin, walked up behind me practically yelling, "Brother Matthews is back there hugging some woman."

After I quieted her down a little, I tried to figure out what she was talking about. I just figured her imagination had been running wild and she had seen someone who looked like Brother Matthews. Maybe she did see him, but didn't recognize Mrs. Matthews. Kay wouldn't agree with any of my explanations of who she had seen, so I asked her to show me.

And there he was with some woman he obviously worked with; I could tell from the uniforms. They were just sitting there talking, in the back of a bookstore, not reading, in a secluded corner... no way! This couldn't be true, another married man in the church, cheating on his wife? I refused to believe that there was anything going on. I told myself I was overreacting.

But, just as I was turning to walk away, he reached over to place his hand on her face ever so gently. He stared into her eyes and then gently kissed her on the lips.

"See, I told jah!" exclaimed Kay.

Oh, my goodness that girl was so loud. I grabbed her up and dashed behind a bookshelf. It felt like all of it was happening to me. I felt as if these men were my husbands. I felt my belief fading. I was frantically questioning why these people, who were hearing the same Word from the same ministers, were doing such bad things. It hurt too much to face it, so I didn't; I buried it, and then put on the mask.

Little by little, I chose to forget. I still attended church on

Wednesday and Sunday, but I started hanging out at night with some friends I had made on campus. They had nothing to do with the church or high school; sometimes they seemed more honest than the people I had trusted with everything. Maybe it was because I never really wanted to know them; I wanted superficiality. I figured the less I knew the better off we'd all be.

I would tell my mom that I had to study at the library or had group sessions with some classmates, anything to keep her from questioning my motives for leaving the house or coming in late.

I became distant and fake, barely speaking to anyone anymore. I would show up just before service began and leaving just before it ended, so I didn't have to talk to anyone. Usually, I would sit in the front row, enjoying every minute of the time I could spend in the presence of God giving him praise. But slowly, I made my way to the back of the church, moving a couple of rows back each week. Eventually, I was gone.

My entire family attended that church; so to explain my absence I made excuses. Excuses soon turned to lies, and before I knew it, I had reverted to my old ways. No matter how bad I wanted to deny the pull of the enemy, my shame, frustrations, anger and regrets would not allow it. I stood at a door to a world that I didn't belong in, a place where chaos and confusion ruled. The lure of freedom from responsibility, freedom from the voices of others, and freedom from the actions of others beckoned me in; so I foolishly entered.

✝✝✝

I felt like it was time for me to move on. I had grown tired of trying to be what others expected. I couldn't pretend any longer. It was time to choose a new path to travel. T-Town (Tallahassee) seemed too close and too many kids from my high school went to school there (including my sister and brother), so that wasn't an option. Atlanta was just as bad; I knew too many people there. I needed to start over somewhere new, where no one knew me. My emotions were unraveling fast, I was reeling, and my mind was a bundle of confusion. I just had to get out of the environment that I was in. I had to go!

My guidance counselor suggested the University of West Florida in Pensacola. It was about two hours up the street, in the opposite direction of everyone else; I was all for it. I didn't even think about it really, I just wanted to leave. So I left.

My mom was worried. She knew there was something wrong, but she didn't question me. She tried to make me go to Tallahassee or Atlanta, because I had relatives in both cities, but after a while, she knew I had made up my mind. Whatever was troubling me, I had to figure it out on my own.

Pensacola was nice. I enrolled in school and found an apartment not far from the campus. I had my first place on my own; it felt good. I was finally free to live my life without asking permission to do whatever it was I wanted to do.

Not long before I left home, I had started dating Brad, a

pretty, white boy with long, curly hair, rosy lips, clear green eyes, and a face of innocence. He had a thing for black girls and I had a thing for anything different from the norm.

I liked Brad a lot; he was honest even when it hurt. We met through Alvin, a mutual friend; boy was he a mess. Alvin was more than flamboyant, he was from the Mediterranean, and everything for him had to be over the top. I met Alvin at the junior college and during my "late night study sessions," we would go to the club or have get-togethers at his apartment out on the beach. I was always the only black face in the crowd.

Anyway, it was a normal "study night" at the club, with loud music, drunken college students, and half-naked girls. I never liked to drink. I mean, I tried to do it, but it wasn't me. Alvin was sloppy by the time I was ready to go, and I had left my car at his house. Brad offered to walk me back to the house because his car was there too. I hadn't met him before that night, but he seemed nice so I agreed.

Small talk, small talk and the next thing I know I'm back at his apartment with my jeans around my ankles. He was nervous; I could feel him trembling when he touched my body and that excited me. He kissed my stomach, his lips quivering in anticipation. Slowly, he made his way down to a place I had almost forgotten. By that time, his nerves had calmed and his lips kissed mine with a passion and tenderness that I had no idea existed. No one had ever done this for me before. I allowed him to explore my body that night, and for the first time sex meant something different to me. It wasn't about love and flowers and fairy tales; it was a raw human emotion that I had never experienced with such intensity. From that moment on, I would never, not experience it again, if I could help it. Brad wasn't my first partner, but he was the first for many things I did. He led me down a path to a world that I was getting very comfortable with.

I had officially turned my back on everything that I held dear. Part of me didn't like it, but another part of me did and it was too easy to do "wrong."

When I moved to Pensacola I left everything behind, including Brad. We were still a couple, seeing each other on weekends, holidays, and anytime we could get away. My phone bill started to get out of hand talking to him so much, but I missed him.

One night, we were both a little too sexually aggravated and talking on the phone wasn't going to cut it. He suggested that we meet at the halfway point in Destin, a small quiet beach town in between the two cities. We met at a spot on the water, where we often stopped to picnic and relax. It was in the middle of the night, in the dead of winter and no one was around. Brad was a free spirit, that's what I loved about him. He wanted to have sex right there on the beach. I was young at the time, thought I was in love and free, so I figured why not.

Being wrapped in a blanket on a beautiful beach in the middle of the night was dreamy, and although I was at a point in my life where I was trying to figure myself out, I felt safe with

Brad. I really liked him. He didn't judge me, and he didn't question my motives; he just accepted what I offered. We talked about his plans after culinary school, and we talked about what I would do after graduating, as we listened to the waves crash against the shore.

✝✝✝

My parents didn't have the money to pay for my education, so I applied for financial aid, loans, and of course, a job. I started working at Hooters, the whitest restaurant I have ever been in. I was the only black person there, besides the cooks, on any given night. I was losing myself and I felt it. Cedric and Gary, two of the cooks there, were my homeboys. I loved those guys, and if they weren't around I don't think I would have made it through my little stint working there. I also met a girlfriend (Melissa) that to this day is the sweetest, most genuine person I have ever met, outside of family. I told my mom I was working at Applebee's, because I knew that she wouldn't approve of me working at Hooters. I hated lying to her. At first it was hard, but soon enough it was easy, just like all the other wrong things I was up to, lies just seemed to flow out of my mouth like water off a duck's back.

Unfortunately, even with financial aid, loans, and the job, I wasn't making it. I had to get a roommate.

Morgan Phillips was a friend from high school who just happened to be attending UWF at the time. Morgan was a little bitty thing; she reminded me of actress, Nia Long. I had no idea she was in Pensacola until I ran into her on campus one day. I was reluctant about asking her to be my roommate because I recalled from high school that Morgan could be moody— even witchy— at times. But, I needed to do something, so I called her up and asked about her living situation. Low and behold, she needed the relief as well. Finally, I had a roommate and a girlfriend to hang out with outside of work.

Morgan didn't hang out too much, but we did manage to have some good times. She was majoring in Education and I was studying Communication, focusing in Public Relations. I wasn't really interested in school, at the time I was just going through the motions.

Morgan had a study partner, Kevin, for one of the classes she was taking. He was cute, had a nice little caboose, and a pretty smile. At first, I thought that he was her boyfriend, because he was studying Medicine, not Education. I couldn't really figure out what classes they would possibly have in common. Both were in their later years of study, so I figured they used studying as an excuse to be together. I guess she figured I would go back home and tell her business, and for the same reason I kept my misdeeds on the low. I trusted her, but you never know what someone will do or say, so I rationed knowledge of where I was and whom I was spending time with.

✠✠✠

Clubbing wasn't Morgan's thing, but when we did hit the streets, we did it right. One Friday night we went out dancing at

Seville Quarter, the place was packed. P-Cola wasn't a very ethnic town— at least as far as we knew—so we were surprised to find so many brothers there that night. We assumed they must have been in the military and they were.

They were in town for a rugby tournament between the Navy and Army; I think it was the Navy and Army. Anyway, that night we met Peter and Robert. They wanted to know if we knew of somewhere else a little more "colorful" to party that weekend. We told them about a few places and promised to meet them at one of them the next night.

The following night, just like we promised, we all met up at a club, but it was practically empty. We didn't let that hinder our fun. We danced and laughed until they kicked us out, but the guys didn't want to go home. We drove around, clowning; we even stopped in the middle of an empty street so Robert could get his dance on. We wandered about until we found a crowd. Thank goodness, it was around the late night food stand with the best fry boxes in the entire city, because we were starving.

These guys were cool; we tripped out and joked around as if we were from the same neighborhood and had known each other all our lives. It didn't even bother me to be eating greasy fried chicken with my hands, sitting on a curb in the middle of the morning. I was having a good time, but Morgan was tired and hinting strongly that it was time to go home. I wasn't ready to leave at all, and the guys were still game to stay up all night, but she drove, so I had to go. Peter convinced me to let him follow us back to our place. Morgan was hot about that, but I paid half the bills, so she could forget about him not coming over; he was coming and that was that.

Morgan got into the car while I hurriedly gave Peter directions, just in case we lost him along the way. I knew she was getting mad and I wanted to calm her down before we got home. After all, I did still have to live with this girl and even if she was tired, she really was having just as much fun as I was a few moments earlier. I didn't understand where her mood came from.

It was as if someone flipped the switch and Morgan became another person.

When I got into the car, the radio was blaring, so I turned it down enough for her to hear me talk.

"What's the matter girl; did Robert say something to upset you?"

"No."

"Then what's wrong, are you just sleepy?"

"I wonder what Brad is doing right now," she says matter of fact.

I know this chick ain't trying to mess with me. You see, this is what I was talking about; never let another chick know too much about your personal business, because all it takes is for them to get in a mood to ruin your rep, your relationship, or whatever.

But two can play that game and just in case Morgan had

forgotten, I reminded her who she was dealing with. I had honestly forgotten about Brad; I was having a good time. I had told myself that I would ***never*** cheat on anyone I was with, in an established relationship. But when confronted with the opportunity, I searched for an excuse to justify what I wanted to do. I wasn't married, Peter wasn't married, and who knows what Brad was doing almost 200 hundred miles away. Besides, what business is it of hers to judge?

"Was that a threat?" I asked sternly. "Because if it was, let me remind you of something. The last time I checked, you had a man back home too, as well as your 'study partner,' Kevin. So, don't even come at me with that self-righteous bull, Morgan. If you feel like messing up your own situation, go right ahead, I'm game."

"You're right," she admitted with frustration, "I don't even know why I'm mad. Look, forget what I said, I guess I'm just tired." She said in a calmer tone.

"Why don't you tell me what's really bugging you," I said.

"It's nothing, really, I'm just tired," she replied.

"Look girl, we have to live together and if Peter coming over tonight is going to upset that, then we need to pull over right now so I can tell him to go back to the base. It's not that important for me to hook up."

"Forget it, I don't mind," she said.

"Are you sure?" I asked.

"Yes, I'm sure," she said.

I was a little apprehensive about trusting her at that point. She had shown her true colors by threatening me, but she knew better than to mess around. If she did, the consequences would have been greater for her, because she had a child with her man and he wouldn't have appreciated another man in the situation, I was sure of it!

When we got to the apartment, Peter gave Robert the keys to the car so he could get back to the base. Peter had noticed that Morgan was a little upset, so he pulled her to the side and asked permission to be there, before Robert drove away. I think she appreciated that, because her attitude completely changed; I was even impressed. We all walked in together. Morgan went to the kitchen, got herself something to drink, and went to her room.

"Goodnight guys." She said enthusiastically.

I promise you that girl had a split personality; she flipped the script on me too quickly, but I learned to ignore it. She never got psychotic, so I figured there was nothing to worry about.

"Goodnight," Peter and I said in unison.

"Jinks!"

We both burst into laughter and out of nowhere, he planted one on me. We had a brief awkward pause then kissed again. I stood and extended my hand, he placed his in mine, and I led him to my bedroom. I don't know when I became so bold; it was almost instinctual. I liked the way it felt, powerful and in control.

Peter saw the stereo on my nightstand and asked if he could turn it on. He flipped through my CD's and put in Luther's, *Your Secret Love*. Why did he have to go and do that?

Peter was an Adonis; he stood 6'1", had a clean-shaven, baldhead, and had the most beautiful, deep-chocolate skin I had ever seen. Every muscle in his body was evident and he must have weighed about 210 lbs. His body was a dream. This was no college boy; Peter was all man.

I sat on the edge of my bed as he insisted on performing a strip tease for me. I watched his every move. He was so seductive, so sexy; he had definitely done this before.

I had to be dreaming. With each layer he removed, my heartbeat accelerated. I'm not a frail woman but when that man dropped his boxers, I think my heart stopped. I'd finally found my answer for that age-old question, "Does size matter?" For me, ladies and gentlemen, it definitely does.

I don't think my heart has ever beat so rapidly. In my head, I started searching for a way out, because I was scared. But part of me wanted to see if I could handle him. I figured if I could, theoretically, have a baby, I could do this. Yeah right.

Peter walked over and, very tenderly, started undressing me. He knew he would have to be gentle and he assured me that he would take his time. I was so nervous when we came together that he had to try to calm me down. His attempts would be futile; I just couldn't take him. I was embarrassed, but I wasn't going to allow him to leave without something to remember. I didn't want him to leave disappointed or frustrated, so I did what I could to satisfy him.

I tried to get up and go to the bathroom afterwards, but Peter pulled me back. He grabbed a towel I had lying by my bed and cleaned himself up. He then straddled me from behind, and began tenderly massaging my back. Luther was still playing in the background, so we just mellowed out and listened for a while. After a few minutes he got up and stood in front of me.

"Can I teach you something?" he asked.

I paused, looked him up and down, and nodded my head. He gently lowered me to the bed as he kneeled down in front of me. He slowly spread my legs, caressed and kissed my inner thighs, and ran his tongue up and down gently biting, almost playing. The closer he got, the more anxious I became, but he toyed with me and I enjoyed it.

"Are you learning anything yet?" he asked as he played.

"No. I'm not...quite... clear as to...what it is I'm...being taught." I replied in broken pauses.

Then, he kissed me softly and I moaned. He paused for just a moment and then kissed me again. I let out an almost inaudible murmur and then all of a sudden, he consumed me with his mouth, working his tongue in ways I could never put into words. I begin to sing like a canary. He took me there, and I was in a state of euphoria. I lost myself in my lustful desires that day, and every day after, the desire to fulfill those passions became stronger and increasingly more difficult to resist. I would either suffer the withdrawal or succumb to its allure. I definitely learned how to sing that night; after all, Peter was an excellent teacher. But that's not all I learned.

I drove him back to the base around 7am; we hugged and said our goodbyes. He left that afternoon for New York, which was home for him.

I thought about Peter from time-to-time after that night, but I never wanted to contact him. He was my first and only true one-night stand. I never heard from him again and that was fine by me. At that point, I had allowed every barrier to fall. I had no shame! I was going to do whatever I wanted to do and I didn't care who knew it. I was so irritated with how I saw so-called Christians living, that I couldn't see clearly how I should live my own life. Should I be good? Should I be bad? Or was there even

such a thing as either one? I didn't know and at the time I didn't

care.

CHAPTER 5
DIRECTION OF THE LAWLESS

School was a pain, but I managed to keep my grades respectable. The first semester I scheduled all of my classes early, you know, so I could get them out of the way and I could have most of my day to do what I wanted. Boy, was that a mistake.

I was never one to go to bed early. I would stay up rearranging furniture, if I couldn't find anything else to do. You'd think I'd have spent that time studying, but I never really had to; I maintained a B average without it.

My first class of the day was Introduction to Mass Communication. It was an interesting subject, but my teacher had a monotone voice and I was always sleepy. Needless to say the two didn't mix.

For the first time in my college career, I had to hit the books or I was going to fail. I never took notes, because I either fell asleep during lecture or didn't show up at all. I crammed for every test, and procrastinated every paper. How I managed to pass that class with a B was, and still is, a mystery to me.

My mom called at least once a week to check up on me, to see how things were going. I told myself that I would never lie to my mom, but when faced with giving her answers that would hurt her, I felt that I had no choice, but to lie.

Soon I began to lie about everything, even stuff that was just unnecessary. I lied about going to church (although I did go, just not as often as I said I did) and I lied about where I worked. My mom didn't even know that I had a boyfriend until about four months into my relationship with Brad. I made up excuses to not come home, so she wouldn't be able to look me in my face when I answered her. She could always tell when I was being dishonest; maybe because I was so terrible at it, when it came to her. When I did go home, I always managed to leave a book back at my apartment, had to get back to finish a paper, or had scheduled myself to work so I had an excuse to miss Sunday morning service.

I loved my mom too much to hurt her, I often cried just thinking of the disappointment she would feel if she knew who her daughter, whom she had raised with the best of intentions, had become. So in my mind it wasn't lying; I was protecting her from the heartache.

✝✝✝

The next time that I saw Brad, he made a detour through P-Cola to see me on his way to visit his parents in Alabama. I'd never met his parents, but I had spoken to his mom a few times on the phone.

She was more liberal than Brad's dad, who was in his mid-fifties, born and raised in a small town in Alabama. I could just see the burning crosses in his past. I honestly didn't know where Brad and both of his brothers got the nerve to date outside their race. I knew that it nearly killed their father to see it. But he loved them, and he was respectful of the choices they made even though he didn't agree with them.

I often questioned what I was thinking back then. I loved Brad for who he was as a person, but there were social issues that made things hard for us. Still, I didn't regret it.

Brad's brothers' dated only Asian women; one of them even moved to China to study. He says it was for educational purposes, but I bet it didn't hurt that his woman-of-choice was readily available. It was weird to see a white man who had no desire to date a white woman and had no problem admitting it.

Brad wanted me to take this trip with him and although I was shaky about meeting his father, I went anyway. His family was very open with one another; it was almost uncomfortable for me to be around them. The visit made it even more apparent that we were raised differently.

His mom asked us if we used protection when we had sex, right in front of everybody! I was shocked. Brad answered very matter-of-factly, "Yes mother." It didn't seem to bother anyone else in the room; there wasn't a break in conversation or activity. To them, this was normal and I was the only one who was shocked. His dad was actually a sweet old man, nothing like what I had imagined; I felt bad for judging him.

I got along with his family just fine, and he often asked about my family. I made excuses about why I never wanted to introduce him to them. I don't know why I didn't; my family accepted anyone, as long as they made me happy. Maybe it was because I was running away from myself and Brad knew nothing of the person I was before we met. He did eventually meet my mom and a few of my girlfriends briefly, and I think that was enough to satisfy him.

The fact that it never bothered me to tell Brad about Peter puzzled me, things like that would have normally sent me into a cocoon of guilt, I was getting callous; people have always trusted me too easily. Now that I was being dishonest, it was working to my advantage.

✞✞✞

My fall semester had ended, but it was Brad's last semester. He was a Culinary Arts student and had completed his training. He accepted a job on a charter boat in Saint Martin or Sint Maarten, for you Islanders, without discussing it with me first. Maybe it was because he knew that I would give him a problem about leaving; he had already made up his mind to go.

He told me not to wait for him; he wanted me to live my life. It was hard to say goodbye, but we did it.

The week before he left, we spent the time together in New Orleans, where he would take his flight out. It was Mardi Gras time and we took full advantage of the festivities. We partied, we ate, and we made love as often as possible until that fateful day.

I drove him to the airport and we sat at the gate waiting for his flight to board. We didn't talk; we just stared at each other, and stroked each other's hair and face. People were staring at us, but we didn't care. We were use to it; we weren't exactly your typical couple.

When his flight was finally called, my heart dropped. I didn't want him to leave. I told him that I loved him and that I would wait for him. He gently kissed me as tears ran down his face and he stood up to go.

"I love you, don't wait," he simply said.

I stood at the window and watched until his plane was out of sight. Then I cried all the way back to Pensacola.

✞✞✞

I had to resume life; school demanded it and my bills had to be paid. So back to work I went. Brad would be gone for eleven months, so I had to keep busy. I piled on the schoolwork and doubled my workload. I stopped going out and I wrote to Brad every other day. That lasted about a month.

Cedric, one of the cooks at work, was always hitting on me. He told me flat out how he felt and he seemed sincere, but I wouldn't give him a chance. Ced was a married man (with a son) and I always told myself that I would *never* date a married man and that promise I was determined to keep.

He had problems. He was too young when he married, he was only twenty-five and his son was three. He had been married for about two years when I met him. I listened to his problems, but I wouldn't budge on my conviction that it was wrong to go there. He had a family and if he wanted to jeopardize that, it wouldn't be with me. The spiritual consequences were too high and I couldn't afford to pay that debt. Little did I understand at the time, I couldn't afford any of the debt that I was accumulating. Cedric was persistent, but no fool. After everything his wife had put him through, by cheating and disrespecting him, he knew better than to play revenge with someone at work. She was nosy and vindictive, and if she thought for one second that I had anything to do with him, she would take it out on me. I, in turn, would take it out on him, so I warned him to leave me alone. Two angry black women are more than most men could ever handle, so he wisely backed down.

I was working on the opposite side of the restaurant from my girl, Julia, and I really didn't like the girls I was stuck with for the night. So, as often as I could, I ran over to her section to hang out with her. On one of those trips, I noticed a brother sitting at a table by himself, eating some wings with a cold beer. I noticed him immediately because brothers didn't really come in there. It was bugging me that I had seen this guy somewhere before, but I couldn't place him.

After about ten minutes, I finally went up to him.

"Don't I know you from somewhere?" I asked, like an idiot.

He looked confused.

Oh no, what have I just done? Now I have to stand here

and make small talk.

"I don't think so," he replied.

I knew that voice. I tried to dismiss it, but I couldn't, so I just stood there and looked at him for a second at the risk of appearing not only like an idiot, but a desperate idiot.

"Are you sure we haven't met, because I rarely misplace a face."

"I think I would have remembered you, if we had met," he says to my boobs.

I keep forgetting where I work; this uniform is a killjoy for me. I never look like this outside of this place. Oh yeah, now I remember.

"Do you know, Morgan Phillips?"

"Yeah, Oh my goodness, you're her roommate right."

"I was her roommate, she graduated and moved back

home, you didn't know that?"

"No, I didn't. We were just study partners for one class we had together. Boy do you look different"

"See, I told you I knew you from somewhere. What were you trying to do make me look like I was trying to pick you up or something?"

"No, I really didn't recognize you."

"Anyway, I have to get back to work. It's Kevin right?"

"Right."

"O.K., see you around Kevin."

All this time I hadn't believed them, and to be honest I still don't. But he said they were only study partners and so did she, so that gave me the liberty to break another NEVER-breakable commandment of mine: never date your girl's ex, no matter how brief their encounter might have been.

That was an unusually long night for me, but I managed to

squeeze two bills out of those cheap people, so I guess it was worth it. After our shift, some of the girls and I decided to go out to the club, for a ladies night out. The girls from work were wild, off the chain. They smoked pot, drank, and rolled on ecstasy. I wasn't into that scene, but I didn't knock them for doing what they had to do to get their party on.

I loved to dance and when we went out, that's how I got high. Tracy, my petite- big bobbed, loud-mouthed friend, was my dancing buddy. She was the only person I knew who loved it just as much as I did. Tracy and I would stay on the stage until we had to either use the restroom or get something to drink. There were two huge speakers overlooking the entire club, which you could dance on and that is the spot where we remained most of the night.

Those spots were reserved for us, but if we stepped away for more than a minute, someone would hop their little hot behind up there. So, we stayed as long as we possibly could. You could feel the vibrations of the music move through your body from those speakers. How could you not get high off of that?

After an hour or so of non-stop dancing, we decided to take a break and go up stairs.

I really loved my girlfriends. That is one thing about me that has never changed, no matter what I chose to do with my life. I believe in friendship and I was committed to them wholeheartedly. I hung with a crazy bunch of ladies, they were wild and care free, but they were so genuine you couldn't help but have a good time.

The girls and I had played enough for the night, so around 2 am; we decided it was time to go. Then, as we were leaving, Kevin walked in. I knew I would see him again, but I didn't think it would be that soon. We noticed each other and he came over. While it's still a subject of debate, as far as I'm concerned, he asked me out, not the other way around.

✞✞✞

Kevin was the perfect booty call, he didn't expect much and he didn't demand my time or presence for idle nonsense. He just accommodated me sexually when I called him and I liked that about him. He was the tall, dark, handsome, and silent type that all women look for, but without all the drama – like jealousy, neediness, and general up keep.

I was at a point in my life where boyfriends and relationships didn't matter to me. I was less concerned about right or wrong than I was about having someone to keep the loneliness away. I was no longer interested in living up to others expectations of me, or in reconciling my belief in Christ with my actions. The negative behavior I had witnessed from the people at church had completely changed my perspective. It had changed me.

I only wore sundresses around Kevin, for obvious reasons. He was the most laid back person I have ever met. Sex was wild, untamed, and animalistic with Kevin. He did things for me sexually as if he was in love with me. He liked the way I responded to him and he had no problem telling me or showing me.

One night, we decided to go out to Diamonds, a club near his house, and I showed up before he was ready. I sat on the dresser and watched him prepare himself. He watched me in the reflection of the mirror and I knew that he could see up my dress. I had come prepared; I wasn't wearing any underwear.

When he was ready, he walked over to me. "Can I have a taste before we go?" he whispered.

Man, I loved what he could do for me. Kevin only added layers to the deception that I fed my mind and my heart about the validity of the lifestyle choices I'd made. He made it harder to find the desire to separate myself from it. It felt so right to do the things that I was doing. How could something that felt so satisfying be wrong?

✞✞✞

I still thought about Brad a lot. I still wrote the letters and sent the postcards. I spent my time with Kevin, to satisfy my carnal needs, but I still loved Brad.

8/16/97

Dear Ali,

Well, I talked to you last night and you sound great! I promise you, you'll see me before you know it. Just keep your time occupied & stay focused with school.

I found out last night that Maggie had a little boy, Gregory Joseph, Aug. 11, '97. That is also my sister Sara's b'day, I know how excited she would have been.

Okay sweetie, just wanted to drop you a line. And by the way, I think the call cost about $2.50 a minute, maybe I can find a cheaper way to call, okay.

Take care & I Love You,

Brad.

Brad and I kept in contact while he was gone; he knew that I was living my life, but I never threw that fact in his face. I knew that he had, similarly moved on. But, we loved each other and when he returned, I expected us pick up where we had left off. So, I did what he suggested; I kept my time occupied.

For the next month, school was a mess. I took on too much of a load, anticipating that I was going to have a lot of free time on my hands. I had signed up for Debate, Public Speech, Public Relations, Western Civilization, and Accounting.

Uhhh!

I was behind on everything, so I had to take two weeks off from work, just to catch up. That, in turn, put me behind on my bills. I was under a lot of stress, so I used Kevin to help relieve it. Sex became an escape for me. No matter what the problem, sex was the answer. To be honest, it wasn't so much the sex, as it was the company. I just wanted someone to occupy my space and chase away those feelings of emptiness that sometimes overwhelmed me. In my naïve mind, sex had to be offered in exchange for his presence.

Kevin's birthday was coming up and he and a bunch of his

friends decided to throw a 70's party to celebrate. I didn't have the time to be going to a party, but I needed a break from the bedroom, so I took it.

I wore a mini dress I had found at the Goodwill. It was green with a bold black stripe down the middle. I flipped my hair, put on a thick black headband, and finished the look off with some platform leather boots. Kevin had on a jump suit like the ones you see the guys wearing in the old seventies movie with Richard Pryor, *Car Wash*. He left the suit open and put on a fly collar, polyester shirt on underneath and topped it off with an Afro wig and killer platforms. My baby did it up! Everybody was dressed up in pink polyester suits, dashikis, black leather, platforms, and brim hats with feathers everywhere. There were more pimps and whores in attendance that night than there was on the stroll last weekend on Hollywood Boulevard. It was dy-no-myte!

After the party, I helped Kevin clean up and load the cars

with all the leftovers. We went back to his place and started our regular routine; we were barely into the house before he was all over me. Foreplay lasted about twenty minutes and when it came time to do the deed, he realized he was out of condoms. I wanted to keep going, but I couldn't. I made him get dressed and go down the street to the convenient store. It was so funny to see him put his costume back on, wig and all, to go up to the store. He said the kids hanging out up there got a kick out of it.

When we were done, I prepared to leave like usual, but for some reason he wanted me to stay. So I did. I don't know why, but that signified the end of Kevin and me. The fun was gone. We were getting used to each other and a relationship was not what I wanted or needed at that point in my life. I already had a man and Brad would be back before I knew it.

✝✝✝

Brad had been gone for a while by then and deep down, I knew the likelihood of us resuming our relationship was slim to none. But I held on; I was still in love with him. The last time I had

talked to him, things hadn't gone so well. I let him know that I was

waiting for him and he didn't respond to me the way he normally

did. But I guess I wasn't listening.

10/25/97

Dear Alicia,

Hey Sweetie, I got your letters over this past week and talked to you two days ago. Thanks for calling on my birthday. We're just getting ready to head out so I'm trying to finish up some letters and postcards. Not much is going on down here. The weather is still hot and work is the same. Well you were asking me the other night if I had "done" anything yet. I feel awkward writing about this to you but yes, I had sex with a Brazilian woman a few days ago. Just another one-night stand that I'm not very proud of. Yes, I did use a condom. Alicia, I don't want you to convince yourself that when I get back to the states that we'll get back together. I hope this doesn't sound too harsh, I don't mean for it to. But if you keep on doing what you write to me in your letters, waiting for me I mean, I think you'll regret it in the future. Please don't be mad at me, Alicia. I just want to be honest with you. Thanks for being my best friend, Alicia. Take care of yourself. Love, Brad

Apparently, I had a way of making him feel guilty about

moving on, even though I had moved on long before he did. I

didn't realize I had been giving him a guilt trip. I had made it seem as if I had been sitting around knitting scarves and baking cookies, while marking the days off of my calendar. I decided to come clean in my next letter.

11/03/97

Hey Baby, it's me. Look I got the impression from your last letter that I had been sending you mixed signals. I love you, I hope that you know that and I do want us to get back together when you come back to the states, I won't lie about that. But I haven't been sitting around counting the days. I met someone to spend my lonely nights with; I hope that doesn't disappoint you. You are my best friend as well and I'm glad to here that you feel the same way. You're a man and you have needs, so while you're away live your life with no concern of me, I don't want you to feel as if you missed something worrying about hurting my feelings. We'll face our future when you get back, but until then have fun because I know I am!
Love,

Alicia

My mom knew me better than anyone did, and she knew that I was waiting for Brad to come back to the states, even though I never mentioned it to her. She always thought I settled for the wrong man and that I sold myself short. I always knew she could tell me what I was feeling, but it never was more apparent to me until I received this letter from her:

Alicia,

How do you expect to have a solid, lasting relationship with someone who doesn't love the Lord? I wish you will just sit down and meditate on young men – the ones you've had in your life, you give too much of yourself. I've told you that before. You don't go out of your way; let him go out of his way. Brad is a nice guy, but not the one for you. The person for you is the one that I've been praying for:

saved

not looking at your beauty

not in night clubs

not drinking

not smoking

cursing

successful

love you for you

go out of his way for you

loves the lord more than he loves you

When you find these qualifications. That's your man! From this day on – focus on God and what he has for you. Don't try to date, just get back to the Lord – with your whole heart and don't wait for Brad to come back for a visit – you're too beautiful on the outside & in – you don't have to do that.

I Love you and I'm praying for you always, so God's not gonna let you settle with nothing less than His best! Yeah!

My mom had a way of bringing me back around, but she didn't know the whole story. I wasn't her precious little girl anymore and I hadn't been living my life according to her standards. I think she knew that I had strayed, but I'm not sure that she knew just how far away I had drifted.

Looking back now, I wish that I had listened to my mother at that moment. I could have saved myself from the unimaginable life that led me to where I am now, a life that I can barely believe I've had. My innocent, youthful mistakes and growing pains, which I thought were deplorable then, were typical mistakes that all young women make during that time in their lives. I was stubborn and proud and like too many of us who had to learn the hard way how *not* to fail, how *not* to mess up, how *not* to make the mistake in the first place, I did things my way and unfortunately, got my results!!!

It was my junior year, and the semester was coming to an end. The Thanksgiving holidays were just around the corner and I couldn't wait to go home to see my family. I had been gone for some time now and I missed them. I didn't care anymore what people thought; I had become comfortable with who I was and I didn't feel the need to explain my actions to anyone.

It's not that I didn't want to go to church, I still believed in the principles that I was taught. I just didn't believe in the people around me. We all fall short, never quite living up to the standards set by others. But I still held bitterness for what Lois and Jason had done, so I kept my distance. I blamed other people for my disposition; I blamed external activities, circumstances, and the actions of others for my attitude. I was in "ME" mode to the 100th degree and nothing or nobody could drag me out of it!

That Thanksgiving was an interesting one, to say the least. Nobody was aware of my lifestyle choices. Either I was still good at hiding them or my family just didn't care to speak on it.

My sister, Felicia, brought her boyfriend, Larry, home for the first time and my brother brought, Novi, his girlfriend again. I was sure those two were headed for the alter. Novi had been dating my brother for a few years now and she seemed to fit right in, as if she had been raised up with us. I considered her a sister already, rather than just another girlfriend.

There was always a big celebration during the holidays; the house was always filled with relatives and friends, laughter and jubilee. Preparing the holiday dinner at my house was always a special time; that's when the ladies of the house, my mom, my sister, my Aunt Lisa, Novi, and any girlfriend that we happened to bring home that year, got a chance to hang out. We were all raised the old fashioned way, to be mothers, wives, and caregivers. That didn't mean it was all that we could or would be, but it would be a part of our character, in whatever future we chose. My mom trained us to take care of our men, not as a chore, but as a sign of respect, loyalty and love; it was our duty.

At first, I had a problem with it because, growing up, the only so called men I had to practice on were my bigheaded brothers and my uncle. I didn't mind my dad, because he was my dad, but my brothers were another story.

They didn't have to do anything; we fixed their plates, cleaned their rooms, washed their clothes, and waited on them, hand and foot. As I got older, I understood a little bit better, because my brothers had their duties as well. They had to keep the yard clean, work (when they were old enough), and they were our protectors. They all turned out to be respectable men, true big brothers, great fathers, and loving husbands, so it was worth it.

This particular year, there were a lot of us in the kitchen: Mom, Felicia, Novi, Lisa, Pam, Cher, and of course, me. No one person had to do a lot. We all had our specialties. Pam and Cher were friends of my sisters from college, so they got to do the grunt work: chopping the veggies, peeling the potatoes, and cutting & washing the greens. My mom definitely had to do the potato salad, dressing, sweet potato pies, lemon cheesecake and red velvet cake. My sister prepared the greens, Novi hooked up the macaroni and green beans, and I had the yams and broccoli casserole. Lisa put her foot in this mean pound cake, and anybody who had the time prepared the rolls.

My dad hooked up the turkey (he smoked it on the grill, so technically he wasn't in the kitchen). We never talked about weighted issues during that time, we just laughed, reminisced, and argued about insignificant stuff like who was going to wash the dishes or put away all the leftovers. We even gossiped a little, it was fun.

After dinner was ready, we all came into the main dining area together to prepare to chow down. We had a lot of people at the table this year, seventeen to be exact. It was a tradition in our house, that each person was given a moment to express what they were thankful for. You know there is always someone in the bunch who just doesn't get it, and when it's their turn to give thanks, they don't know what to say. There's this awkward silence, as they wait for us to pass them by and go on to the next person in line. I always thought that was funny.

Felicia didn't eat very much that afternoon; she had an upset stomach. It was strange, because I thought that girl's stomach was made of steel; usually she could eat anything.

When the men were done, like clock work, they got up from the table without touching a thing and headed straight for the living room to watch the game. Cleaning up was not pretty after seventeen people just ate a huge meal like that, but it had to be done. Thank God, we had a lot of help that year.

My mom was in the kitchen trying to find a home for all the leftovers, and my sister was sitting at the counter, watching. Larry, my uncles, my brothers, two of my cousins, some friends, and I were in the living room watching the game. I was surprised no one was asleep. I hated football, so I left the living room and ventured to the kitchen to see what was going on in there.

When I walked in, I must have caught the tail end of a conversation, because all I heard was, "I'm pregnant," coming from my sister Felicia.

So that explained the stomach problems. My mom froze. She couldn't speak, she couldn't move, and I'm not sure if she was even breathing.

I looked back into the living room, to see if anyone had heard what my sister had just said. I guess there was a commercial on, because it appeared as if they did.

Larry looked surprised, as if this was news to him too. My brothers were looking at him, like it was time to have a talk. I asked my sister if she was serious and she said, "Do you want to see the WIC checks?" I couldn't help but to laugh.

My mom wanted all of us to be married and settled before we had children. She was hurt to hear the news, I could tell by the look on her face, but, after the initial shock wore off, she was O.K. (I think).

I don't know what happened after that, I left to go on my annual dessert pick-up. The dessert pick-up is when you go visit friends who are in town for the holiday, talk for a while, and eventually make your way over to their dessert table. You pick up a few slices and move on, as if you didn't already have enough food at home. It was fun and a tradition that we all participated in.

My mom and sister talked, I'm sure, but I didn't want the pressure of Mom's expectations of my childbearing time schedule adding to my own guilt. I guess I just didn't want her to question whether I was doing anything to get pregnant myself, so I chose not to participate.

I had always assumed that I was the only one out there doing things my mother would disapprove of, but it seems that my road wasn't the only one that needed a street sweeper to run through it. I'm sure my sister doesn't regret getting pregnant; she was twenty-four and she felt it was time for her to start a family, even though she didn't exactly do things "in order."

Being my mother's daughter was too much pressure sometimes. To me, she was Mrs. Susie homemaker, the model for all mothers and wives, and everyday I felt myself falling short of the glory. She didn't yell, didn't demand, or command anything of us. She led by example, only hoping and praying that we would do what was right. Sometimes, I wish she would have forced her wishes on us, been unbearable, or even a little stubborn, but she was none of those things. I spent the bulk of my life trying to protect her from the daughter I had become.

✟✟✟

The semester finally ended. It had been a rough one, and I didn't want to do that again. I decided to take a break from college; I was only there because I thought that's what everybody expected me to do and I was tired of trying to live up to everyone else's expectations. I was going to do me for a change.

Then came the big question: who was I?

I was coming up with nothing.

As I sat there trying to figure out who the heck I was, my phone rang and it nearly scared me to death. I didn't get very many phone calls, maybe because I didn't have very many friends, outside of family, and I had just left all of them at home.

"What's up?" I would know that voice anywhere.

"What's up girl, how are things going in San Antonio, Texas these days?" I asked.

It was my girl Stephanie; we went to high school and part of college together. College wasn't her thing, so she had dropped out and joined the military. I always admired the fact that she did what she felt like doing, seeming not to care what people thought of her.

"Great, when are you coming down for a visit?" she asked.

I always told her I would come visit if she ever got close enough for me to drive and San Antonio was about a twelve hour drive away. Right then, that didn't seem very close.

"Shoot girl, you live too far away."

Oh, here we go.

"I never said that when I came down to visit you guys, now did I?"

She always tried to use that old excuse.

"You were coming home to see your daddy and brother, we just happened to live in the same city, so stop trying to make it seem like you did us all of favor by coming home for the holidays. By the way, where were you on Thanksgiving? I went by your dad's to get my sweet potato pie and he said you decided not to come home. But he didn't tell me why. Is everything all right?"

She paused for a second, so I knew she was either about to lie or drop a bomb on me.

"Well, since you asked, I got out of the military about a month ago and decided to stay here in San Antonio, I just started a new job about two weeks ago and I couldn't get the time off."

What did she just say?

"What do you mean you got out of the military, you just got in? What did you do this time?"

She paused again.

"Are you coming to visit me or not?"

That girl was crazy, I knew she had done something wrong, but I wasn't going to press the issue.

"Let me see if I can get the time off and I'll call you back," I replied.

"O.K. Bye!" she said.

"See, Ya!"

I thought, maybe I should go. It's not like I was doing anything around here anymore.

'RIIIIING!'

My goodness, I have to turn the blasted ringer down on that phone or I'm going to have a heart attack up in here!

"Hello."

"Hey baby, Kevin. Why don't you swing by here and see me?"

"When, now?"

"Yeah, now," Kevin said.

This was strange. Kevin never called me in the middle of the day like that. Shoot, he had never called me at all. He was my booty call; I wasn't his.

I decided it didn't matter. I had been planning to call him later on anyway; I had just been waiting for the sun to go down.

"Sure, give me about an hour or so I have to run some errands," I said.

I couldn't let him think I was just sitting around doing nothing.

I often did things that didn't make sense. I had already broken things off with Kevin, and I could have gone on without ever calling him again. But, the fact that he reached out to me threw me off, and to be honest, at the time, what he could do for me was just what I needed.

"About an hour?" He asked.

"Yeah, about an hour, is that O.K. with you or do you have something or someone else to do?" I said.

I had never questioned him before, so why was I questioning him then? I didn't care what he did.

"No, I just wanted to see you now. I've been waiting for you to get back from visiting your family and I guess anticipation makes my manhood grow harder."

"Well, since you put it that way, I guess my errands can

wait."

I think I took advantage of anyone who showed any sign of what I considered weakness, and Kevin's laid-back demeanor was just that. However, when he showed the least bit of assertion, I responded almost instinctively. I loved the bad boys, like so many other women, they would be my Achilles heel.

✝✝✝

I was getting antsy, it was time to make another move, but I had to wait for Brad to come back before I made any major decisions; my life was getting too routine. All I did was work and hang out and I was bored with that.

My manager at work had a friend who needed some models for a print ad and he told the guy about me. I had considered being a model once before, but I didn't know how to go about getting into the business, so I decided to check this guy out. We met at the restaurant with my manager and he explained what the job entailed. It was $1,500 for one print ad. At the time, I thought that was great, so I took it. I didn't realize I would see that ad everywhere for years to come and not make a dime from it, because I gave them the rights to the photos. I didn't do any more modeling while I was in Florida, but the bug had bitten me and I wanted more.

The Christmas holidays were right around the corner and I planned on spending two weeks at home, so I could do most of my shopping with my family. We always waited 'til the last minute. Just before I left my apartment, I decided to check the mail one last time. I was glad that I did, because I had gotten my Christmas card and letter from Brad a little earlier than I had expected.

Dear Alicia,   *12/06/97*

I know that I tell you this probably every other time I write to you, but can you believe that I've been down here four months? You know what they say, time really flies when you're working you're a** off, and you never have any free time, and even though you're living in the Caribbean you're still white as a ghost and.... I'm sorry, I'm rambling. Well, you'll never guess who's coming to St. Maarten, Wyclef and the Refugee All Stars. And unless some *miracle takes place, I'll be on this da** boat while they are performing. Just my bad luck I guess. Hey, I've got some questions for you, you can answer them for me the next time you write: 1. did you receive the last letter that I sent?, it had some phone cards in it and some money to help you pay the phone bill - 2. how's school going? (grades, almost finished, etc.) –3. any new boy toy prospects? (ha-ha) – 4. you gotten those braces off yet? Well sweets, I hope you have a great Christmas with your family. I'm still planning on coming home in the middle of March. I'm counting the days until I'm through with my job (70 to go!). Hope to hear from you soon. Take Care of Yourself.*

Love,

Brad

P.S., Give your mom my best and tell Lois and Stephanie I said

hello.

It was good to hear from him. We've shared more while apart than we did when we were together. I was definitely better at conveying my feelings when not faced with an immediate response, and it became more apparent over time, that he was the same way.

The drive home was beautiful. I always waited to leave at dusk, because I was more alert at night. This trip I decided to take my time and soak up the scenery.

The stretch between the two cities was sparsely populated. It was mostly wooded areas; a few strip malls, an apartment complex here and there, and some of the world's most beautiful beaches. When you're born and raised in a city, you seldom appreciate its beauty until you are taken away to see how the rest of the world lives. I didn't realize what I had there; all I knew is that I wanted to be somewhere else. Anywhere, but where I was.

On this particular drive, I noticed a flea market to the right of the highway. Good for me it was still open. I'd always been a sucker for a flea market. I got that from my aunt, who could find the most bedazzling bargains in the midst of the biggest piles of junk. I hoped to be as fortunate to one day find that hidden treasure that no one, but me, could see. I couldn't believe that I had never seen it there before, but I'd been too consumed with the drive ahead of me to pay attention.

I pulled off the highway and turned into the parking lot of the market with a heightened anticipation of my hunt. The lot was unpaved and dust was flying everywhere, so much so, that I almost turned around. It took a few minutes to find a parking space, but when I finally did, I opened the door to a God-awful stench.

"What is that smell?" I said out loud to myself.

I tried to shrug it off and keep moving towards the market, but I couldn't take it. I practically had to run back to my car and sped off. It was as if the cops were after me. I high-tailed it down the road for about ten miles before I was able to escape that putrid odor.

I began to laugh hysterically. I kept picturing myself running back to my car and speeding off from that flea market like I was on the Dukes of Hazard. I was laughing so hard that I started to tear up. I could barely breathe and I was swerving all over the road, so I was forced to pull over.

When I gathered myself and cleared my eyes, I realized where I was, Destin. It was the very same spot that Brad and I had come to time and time again, to picnic and relax. Just a year ago, we made love on that very same stretch of beach.

I decided to take a stroll by the water. It was a peaceful evening. The waves were pounding back and forth, as a slight breeze kissed the air. It was strange that way sometimes, in that part of Florida, it didn't really get cold during the winter. I was blessed with such a night.

I recalled the night Brad and I had been there the previous winter; we sat on a large sand dune, planning our future together. We had this oversized down comforter wrapped around us and we had snuggled and talked until the sun came up. I missed him a lot; we really did have some special times.

The ocean is so amazing, so majestic, and so alive. When I closed my eyes, I could hear its heartbeat. It's slow, strong, steady pulse, it's consuming and intoxicating embrace. I sat there for a moment, soaking it all in, remembering how awesome and amazing and breath taking God is. Life's worries seemed so insignificant in that moment, a moment that I wanted to preserve for as long as I could. It passed so quickly, as if I blinked and it was over. So much had passed by just as quickly: my childhood, my time with CJ, church, not to mention my friendship with Lois. As I looked to the sky that night, I released a bellowed sigh while noticing a deep shade of blue/black shining down on me. It reminded me of something familiar and it triggered a response that was personal and hurtful. I couldn't immediately recall what it was, but as I sat there, the memories came flooding back to me. I couldn't face the memories then, not that night, so I shrugged it off.

I missed the church, the fellowship, and the presence of God— *No*, it wasn't the church I missed, it was the feeling of being surrounded by peace, love, warmth, and serenity; that's what I missed. I felt Him there, on the beach, all around me. Why was it so hard for me to just go back? Maybe it was because I didn't know what I would be going back to. I didn't miss the physical church, you know, the structure of brick and wood. But, I did long for the spiritual church and the people who had a heart towards God. I missed those who loved Him with an all-consuming love and who ushered in His presence with a true faithfulness. I missed that; I missed it a lot.

I knew He would forgive me, if I just asked, but I wasn't sure what I would be asking forgiveness for. Did I forsake the assembly? Did I turn my back to Him? I knew that I hadn't lived my life according to scripture day in and day out, but my love never changed, the passion that I had for Him never changed; in my private moments He was still God and I honored that, in my heart.

I considered that perhaps my privacy had become my prison. I had more questions than I had answers right then and it was all too much to digest in that moment. I needed to get back on the road, if I ever planned to make it home and I wasn't going to solve anything, much less everything, that night.

I stood and brushed the sand from my clothes, wiped the tears from my eyes, took one last gaze, then turned and walked away. The rest of the drive was uneventful, I didn't turn on the radio and I didn't make any more stops, I just drove.

✝✝✝

When I got to the house, there was no one there; I guess they got tired of waiting on me. There was a note on the table from Novi stating:

We got tired of waiting on you **so we left, be back soon and don't eat my cake!!!!!!!!!** *Love ,Novi*

Where that girl learned to write was a mystery. The note looked as if Kay, my three-year old cousin, had written it.

I was right, they did get tired of waiting, but that was for the best. I needed to get some rest before tackling the ravaging Christmas crowd. Novi and my brother were officially engaged at that point. He had done everything right too, just as he was

taught. He had called her dad without her knowing, and asked for

her hand in marriage, just before Thanksgiving. Novi had spent

the past two years with us for the holidays, so after they left our

house for Thanksgiving, my brother suggested that they go by and

see her folks. They lived in a small town on the way back to

Tallahassee, so it didn't seem out of the way. Novi appreciated

that my brother had considered that she wanted to see her

relatives. When they got there, everybody was still at her

grandmother's house: cousins, uncles, aunts, sisters, brothers

and, of course, Dad and grandma. Novi thought it strange to see

everyone still there. It was late and the crowd would have been

usually been sparser by then. But she was happy to see them all,

so the thought quickly cleared her mind. As soon as they walked

in, she was surrounded by family offering hugs and kisses and

didn't see as my brother dropped to one knee behind her. When

she reached a relative my brother hadn't yet met she reached

back to grab him. But he wasn't there. She turned around and clasped her hands to her face when she realized what was going on. She found him on one knee, in front of her with his hand extended to hold hers. Tears rolled down her cheek, he eloquently spoke,

"I love you with everything in me and you would do me the greatest honor by becoming my wife. Zenovia White, will you marry me?"

He had barely gotten the last word out of his mouth before she responded with an exuberant, "Yes, Yes, Yes!" There was a spontaneous rumble of clapping and jubilation from the kinfolk. He had done it right, and that made me proud. Novi loved telling us that story and I loved hearing it every time; it was a fairy tale proposal, the one that I hoped for when my time came.

I decide to take one of the upstairs bedrooms for a change; it was nice and quiet, away from all the traffic of the holidays. Normally I'd rather be downstairs because the chaos, the crowds, the traffic were what made the holidays, the holidays.

The phone was ringing while I was walking up the stairs and I was in no rush to get to it. When I got to the room, I couldn't seem to find the phone anywhere. After several minutes of searching I finally found it sitting on the desk right in front of my face. I must have been more tired than I thought. It began to ring again and I ignored it, thinking it couldn't be for me. But, moments later it was ringing again and my plan had been to ignore it, but after three or so rings I changed my mind. By the time I picked up the receiver, whoever it had been, had hung up. I forgot that my mom's phone rang constantly.

"Riiiiing."

I assumed by then, that whoever was calling really needed to get in touch with someone. I didn't want to listen to that phone ring all night, so I reluctantly answered.

"Hello," I said.

"By chance is Sister Davis in?" The voice on the phone

asked.

"No, she's out shopping, but she should be back soon," I replied.

"Is this Sister Alicia?"

Oh no, it's Pastor Froman! I knew I shouldn't have answered this thing. What do I say? Please Lord don't let him sense that I've been doing wrong, I promise I'll start acting right, Please!

I laugh now, when I think about that moment. We always seem to know exactly who God is when we are in a tight spot.

"Hey, Pastor Froman, yes sir it's me."

"Well it's good to hear your voice we haven't seen you around in a while, how's everything going in school?"

"Everything's great, I got my grades back for this past semester and I got a 3.4"

Why did I say that? I got a 3.2. I didn't have to lie about that, and to the Pastor. Lord, please don't strike me down!

"Have you found a church yet?"

Think fast Licia! What's the name of that pastor from the TV commercial you saw back in P-Cola? Think fast!

"Oh, yeah, a good one. It's almost like our church here, just a larger congregation," I replied.

"Really, what's the pastor's name? I might know him; I go down there from time to time."

Licia think girl, O.K., breath don't panic.

"You do? I didn't know that."

Oh, I remember!

"My Pastors name is Pastor Taylor, at Faithful Covenant, do you know that church?"

"No, I can't say that I do, maybe I'll check it out on my next visit."

"That would be nice, a familiar face in the crowd. By the way, how are Mrs. Froman and Gary doing?"

"Great. Doing the Will of God, so we're all doing well. Make sure to tell your mom to call me when she gets in."

"I will."

"Thank you ma'am."

"You're welcome."

We said goodbye simultaneously and hung up. I knew I was going to Hell after lying to the Pastor.

Christmas whirled by without much fanfare; the folks were the same. There was fusing and fighting, eating and rejoicing, but I got some much needed time to relax. I even got a chance to finish reading a novel I had started at the beginning of the school year, thanks to an empty house.

CHAPTER 6
A THIN LINE

It was the spring of 1998, Brad had returned from the islands. Kevin was falling in love, and Hell had unleashed its fury on my life. I had anticipated Brad's return to be a joyous one. I had taken off from work, bought a nice racy, white negligee, and a black mood light. When he arrived at my apartment, he appeared genuinely happy to see me and I was certainly happy to see him. When I saw him again after such a long time, I forgot about all the wrongs that I had committed against him and our relationship. In effect, I acted as if my stuff didn't stink. We laughed and talked about old times for hours, recalling all the good and the bad that created the most unlikely pair. I fell in love with him all over again. His inability to pretend to be anyone other than himself was the most attractive force, so when he placed his hand on my face and began to kiss my lips, I gave in eagerly.

Brad didn't stay that night. He had to return to Mobile, where he was visiting with his mother. She expected him to return that night and he didn't want her to worry.

As soon as daybreak surfaced, I called Kevin to let him know that things were over between us. I told him Brad had returned and in so many words, I had no need for him sexually anymore. I told him I wanted to remain friends. He didn't take it well. I instantly went from being his boo to being a sell out, choosing a white boy over a brother. He was angry and wanted nothing more to do with me. He told me to go to Hell and hung up in my face. I was hurt, for a moment, but my focus was on Brad so I dismissed Kevin with little fanfare.

Later that evening, I called Brad to find out why he hadn't called me all day, and he didn't even hesitate to let me know that it was over between us. I was shocked into a state of disbelief.

He'd moved on while he was away. He said he didn't want to hurt me, but for the life of me, I couldn't figure out how he was trying *not* to hurt me. Brad always had a problem with confrontation. He would just rather not deal with them at all and that was what he was doing at that moment. I wasn't about to let him off the hook so easily.

"Why is it over, what's going on Brad?"

"Look Alicia, you know I don't want to hurt you and I'll always love you, but I can't do this."

"You told me you would never hurt me Brad, why are you doing this to me?"

As I spoke, my voice began to crack, and the tears began to flow. My heart ached and my head was pounding. I was doing my best to keep from loosing control, when he just hung up on me. Shock ravaged my body and rage began to germinate somewhere deep in my soul. Somewhere between pain and forgiveness, I can attest that insanity lives. Before I knew what had happened, I was standing outside his bedroom window, soaked from the rain. I had a butcher knife in my right hand, but I had no idea how I got there. When the reality of what I was doing struck me, I broke down, sobbing hysterically, and screaming to the heavens. I needed to know why was this happening to me.

My emotions exploded so loudly that it woke up Brad. He rushed outside with a blanket, scooped me up, and took me inside. As he rushed to get me out of my wet clothes, the knife fell from my hand. The look on his face had so much compassion and concern, that all rage was released from my body and I fell limp into his arms. We just cried and held each other until I passed out in his arms. The next morning I woke to breakfast in bed and a note on the pillow next to me.

"I love you more than anything, but I bring out the worst and the best in you and I could never live up to the expectations that you have of me, you're the most beautiful woman I have ever known and my intentions were only to love you, but I've messed that up for us now. When I was on the island, I slept with a woman who is now carrying my child and I could never ask you to accept

that because you deserve more, and more is what you will have without me. No matter what you say, I won't change my mind. I have to go away, you can stay at my apartment as long as you'd like, I'll be at my mothers until you get yourself together.

Please don't hate me Alicia, I'm sorry, and I love you."

I was devastated. I would have given my everything to have just one more night with him. I felt like I couldn't possibly go on without one more moment spent in his arms, with the soft caress of his skin or the kiss from his sexy lips against my flesh. How could he not want to be here right now? What woman could give him more love, more tenderness, more passion than I could? I couldn't understand it, and although I didn't want to let him go, I had no choice. I understood his pain, I understood his need to move on, I didn't want to accept it, but I had to.

I stayed there for days, going in and out of pain, in and out of sorrow, in and out of love, in and out of disgust, and in and out of his belongings. It didn't take me long to realize that I didn't even know this man. After dating for two years, it only took me two to three days to realize that I was in love with an ideal, in love with make believe. I had created this perfect person in my mind and he didn't exist in my reality. We didn't like the same music, didn't like the same clothes, food, or people. We didn't even like the same movies. He loved to read science fiction and I hated it with a passion. He was a drinker who loved to surf and dive. I didn't even like to get my hair wet. I was stunned at how distraught I had become, how ridiculous I had acted over a man I never even knew. In that moment, I vowed to never get into another relationship. I would never let a man take from me what I had no right to give him and he had no right to have. My spirit, my heart, my soul belonged to God, and back to God I would give them. I had no more energy and I had forgotten how I had ended up there in the first place. I took a shower, picked up my keys, and drove home.

✝✝✝

When I got back to my apartment, I was exhausted. But, I also was young and directionless, so I packed my bags, cleaned out my refrigerator, called my girl in San Antonio, and told her to look out for me, because I was on my way. It was a twelve-hour drive, and the only stops I made were for gas and a snack or two. Before I knew it, I was there.

My girl Steph, was mad cool. She did stuff that most people in their right mind would never do. She was a free spirit, lived life to the fullest, always seemed to be having fun, and I was jealous of that. But no more! I was going to live my life like she did. I let my inhibitions loose, and for once in my life I was having a good time for me, not for anyone else, not for a man, not for Steph, not for the crowd, but for me. I wanted to know what I was missing; I wanted to know what it felt like truly to not care what others thought of me. I wanted, more than anything, to know what it meant to be wild and free.

I hadn't seen Steph in some years, and when she opened the door, shock was evident in my bugged out eyes and gaping mouth. Her boobs almost slapped me in the face, her stomach was showing from the very edge of her breast to the very line of her panties —at least where her panties would have been, if she had been wearing any. The skirt she wore could barely be called that. Don't get me wrong; she was working that outfit. Steph's body was banging; and if you have what it takes to wear something like that then by all means, get your wear on. The old me would have been very judgmental at the sight of such boldness, but she was my girl, and I was tired of being that person, so I left it alone. Besides who was I kidding with the situation I had just left with Kevin, Brad and not to mention Peter. I had no rights to call anyone to the carpet about lifestyle choices. We were all on a journey to self discovery and as rocky as it was for me at that time in my life I was willing to go even deeper into a world I had no business in for the sake of my feelings!

"It ain't that bad, close your mouth." Steph said with an amused tone..

The last time I saw Steph was at a Wednesday night church service, the day before she entered the military. I'd always thought that the reason Steph went to church as often as she did, was for the love of Carlos she always changed directions for man in her life. Whatever his interest was became her interest. Fred was heavy into the gym, so when she dated him, she was one physically in shape woman. Greg was into cars, so she learned to replace an engine. Carlos was a preacher-raised, church boy, so off to church she went. Now she was seeing Chris, a dancing fool that hit every club in the city as often as he could, so off to the clubs she went, looking like the typical club hoochie. I wasn't phased; I was ready for anything, and if partying was on the menu, that's what I would have.

It came as no surprise to me that the girl lived right across the street from the club. People were even parking in her driveway to get there. I had little expectation for what would go on that first night, I just wanted to get out of the house and have a little fun. Steph was the most sociable creature on earth, she knew everyone, and everyone seemed to know her. I could never be that way, so being there with her made it easier for me to just let loose and be free. After a half an hour, and twenty introductions, I didn't feel so much like a stranger. I had a good time that night, but it nothing to write home about. At least, not until right before we left. There was one more introduction that had to be made. Alex Slater was an ex-pro basketball player, living in the city at that time. Although the introduction was focused on him, I was focused on his friend. Surprisingly, Steph didn't seem to know the man standing next to Alex, and Alex failed to introduce him, but he was all I saw and the only thing I cared to remember from the entire trip. I returned to Florida to get my affairs in order.

Even though I had just made a vow to God that I would never give away what was *not* mine to give, I just wasn't strong enough to keep my promise. I really wanted to live right, but there was no strength left in me to fight off temptation. I stood at a door that led to shear chaos, and opening it was inevitable for me. I was angry, bitter, resentful, hurt, and confused.

CHAPTER 7
LETTING IT RIP

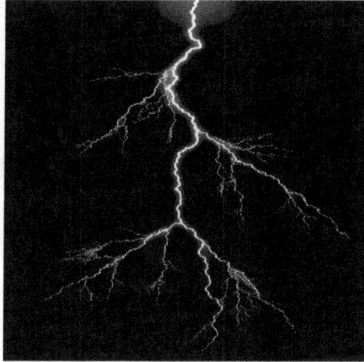

Stephanie had invited me to move to San Antonio a few months prior to my trip. I made the decision to go just as impulsively as I had with the other major decisions I'd made in recent years. I was still running from myself. I needed my life to start making sense and whatever I could change I did. I kept manipulating my surroundings hoping it would get better. So, in the summer of 1998, I packed up everything that would fit into my Mitsubishi Eclipse, gave everything else away, and drove off to San Antonio. I was determined to be free: no ties, no guilt, and no drama!

Yeah right! Within days of arriving to San Antonio, my girl Steph and I were out in the streets partying. I was young, beautiful, and my body was amazingly attractive to the opposite sex. I knew that I had the power to control men with sex. In the past I had shied away from it, but the situation with Kevin and Peter opened me up to being more bold with it, so in San Antonio I started to take the upper hand and used it to my advantage. I wasn't going to be the sucker this time.

I had met Keilan at the very first club I went to in San Antonio, during my first visit, and I recognized him from that night. He was charismatic, flashy, cocky, confident, and bold. Keilan was a bad boy and he made it known right up front. A normal person, with an ounce of sense, would have walked away after hearing what this man had to say. But I had to learn my lesson.

I put myself out there as this tough chick, but the reality was I was faking my way through it. I was immediately attracted to Keilan, and after my breakup with Brad and my arrangement with Kevin, I felt like I needed to be with someone.

The truth is I just didn't know how to be alone. From the beginning, Keilan and I were up front and blunt about what we wanted the relationship to look like, and I use the term relationship very loosely here. I was still a silly girl, green to many things. I thought that I was more skilled at much more than I realized. I believed that I was smarter than the average girl; I believed that I could handle the decisions that I was making.

I remember the night I sat across from him at IHOP. The lights were bright, in fact too bright, for that time of morning. Most of the patrons were fresh out of the bar scene, many of them inebriated from the nights choice of spirit intake. And although the roaring noise of chatter and laughter mixed with the distant symphony of pots and pans clanking, bacon sizzling on the grill, cash registers opening, closing, beeping and slamming, I felt cocooned in his presence. I was more aware of that moment than I have ever been aware of anything in my life. These words that I was about to hear, had to be spoken and I had to except them in order for my journey to shift.

"Do you know what you're getting into, do you know who I am?" Keilan asked me.

"No, who are you?" I smugly replied.

"I'm the man your momma warned you about, I'm the devil in disguise!" he said.

"Oh really?" I giggled.

He was dead serious; he knew he was a manipulator, a womanizer, a cheater, and a liar. He owned it 100 percent. The intensity of his answer still resonates with me today. I can't imagine where my mind was or why I thought it was ok to accept what he said. Nevertheless, I brushed it off as if he hadn't said it. I should have walked away at that moment, but I stayed. It was the beginning of a journey that I now believe I had to take.

In the beginning, he didn't lie to me, but his honesty was

brutal and his truth was not something that most women would want to hear. I was supposed to be just another notch on his belt and at the time, I was content with that. I was a good-looking, intelligent girl from a God fearing family. I was raised in church and I knew better, but I didn't care enough or know enough about myself to even pause to consider the gravity of my decision to be with him. I had no clue what I was doing; the girl that entered into this unholy contract was broken, yet I know now that God was with me!

At first Keilan and I didn't spend much time together. We saw each other whenever either of us needed a fix. I was good with that, because I didn't want anything serious. I wasn't a social butterfly like Steph, so I spent a great deal of my time at home reading, writing, or watching TV.

I tried to be the bad girl, but my true identity was always presenting itself and Keilan took notice. He saw the innocence in me and something in him wanted to preserve that for himself.

Soon our arrangement of "do whatever you want" turned into one of jealousy and controlling behavior. He didn't want me to spend time with anyone, but him. He poisoned my mind against the few girlfriends I'd made in my short time in the city. He intentionally went after them with sexual advances, and many of them succumbed to him. This really messed me up in the trust department, as if I wasn't already broken enough.

The icing on the cake was the fact that Keilan had a girlfriend! Yes, a girlfriend. I discovered that she lived with him after we had been seeing each other for about three months. It was a confusing revelation; because Keilan was never at home and briefly I questioned the seriousness of their relationship, seeing as how they were almost never together. After about eight months, he dropped a bombshell on me. He intentionally waited until I had gotten comfortable with us being together, and I'd chosen to be exclusive to him and him alone. He had started paying my bills, giving me shopping money, taking me on trips, and spending a great deal of his free time with me. Then, he announced the birth of his son – I was blindsided!

Yes, I knew about her, but Keilan had drastically misrepresented her role in his life. He admitted to me that she had already been pregnant when I'd met him. He told me the relationship they had was a business arrangement, because he had given up on the hope of ever meeting someone that he truly connected with. His need to have a child with the "right" girl was no longer priority! He told me that he had just wanted to find someone that met his standard of physical beauty. Emotional fulfillment was no longer necessary for him, because he had realized he couldn't have it all.

Keilan was an anomaly; he was a young, black, wealthy, and influential individual. He marched to the beat of his own drum; he could care less what people thought about him. He had made me feel that I was the most important person in his life. Then he gut punched me with this news and explained it away as a responsibility that he had to honor. He told me that I was the one he fell in love with, that I was the one that met his emotional and physical needs, and that I was the one he had been waiting on. His impatience had gotten in the way.

He said, "I knew that as soon as I made the decision to settle down, I would find the woman I truly wanted to marry."

I was a sucker to fall for such a blatant lie, but I wanted what he said to be true.

That day there was a shifting in my ability to discern the difference between right and wrong, that day justifications, rationalizing and lying to myself became commonplace. I told myself that they only had a relationship of convenience; they weren't married. I was hesitant to stay with him, but it was ultimately easier to convince myself it was okay than it was to walk away.

I had always believed, with all my heart, that there were certain lines that I would *never* cross, but the deception in my heart played me like a fiddle. I was walking a mile in another man's shoes and I did not like the journey; I did not like the

journey!

Years before, I had judged Lois harshly for her choices. I

expected her to make better decisions, but I didn't know where

she was coming from at all. I had no idea why she did what she

did, I had no idea what Jason had whispered in her ear, I had no

idea of the lies her heart had told her, but I judged anyway. I had

condemned her, written her sentence, and ended our

relationship. She had been my best friend; I had loved her and

trusted her with my secrets. But when she'd shown herself to be

human, I just walked away with my self righteous behind!

In San Antonio, God had presented me with the same

choices Lois had had to face. I wanted to blame my choices on

someone else. I felt confused and I was operating blindly. My

relationship with Keilan was very public; we hung out at the clubs

together, went out to eat together, and traveled together. I went

to games and met his friends. I knew where he lived and he came to my place. It was a well-orchestrated lie he had designed especially for me. It had been a strategic plan that he executed well to convince me I was *the* woman in his life. In reality, he had two lives; I dare say he had several scenarios set up with multiple women.

I wasn't special; I was just a possession that he didn't want anyone else to have. He was a spoiled little kid unwilling to part with the toys he rarely played with.

Keilan and I had a volatile relationship. He mesmerized me, and my feelings were all entangled in his rhetoric; no matter what he did or said, it only took a few days to forget why I had been so angry with him in the first place. Even if I'd wanted to go, this was not the type of man you just broke up with: he was a 6ft – 185lb muscular, Mandingo-type brother who was educated, successful, wealthy, and handsome. Maybe, if he didn't know all of that, he would have made someone a halfway decent mate.

Keilan was smug, arrogant, and cocky. He flaunted his

wealth and his influence. He was a very flashy guy. He traveled

first-class, ate at the finest restaurants, and rubbed shoulders

with the rich, famous, and powerful. He made me feel lucky just

to know him, much less be with him. The confident fearless girl

that had left Florida on an adventure was fading away. The girl I'd

been had vanished.

But, at some point, I was supposed to use my intellect. I

thought I was smart, tough, and experienced in matters of the

heart. However, if I had been, I would have heeded the warning

signs and walked away. I should have paid attention to the

feelings of pain, disgust, anger, fear, and betrayal. It's not like he

was my first relationship. I had seen so much dishonesty between

couples and watched so many people close to me in pain – I

should have known better. But, the lies of others, that I had taken

so personally back then, were becoming my own reality and I

knew it. I felt powerless to resist going there; I felt drawn into this

life by a force greater than myself. I'm not saying the devil made me do it, or that God had a hand in it, I just succumbed to my emotions, plain and simple.

In retrospect, the signs were so obvious, like neon lights around every corner, at every stop, in every mirror. He might as well have had a sign flashing above his head: "Dealing with me is like dealing with the devil," at all times!

He'd said it more than once and each time my inner voice yelled at me to get out, but I didn't listen. I wanted him and nothing would stand in my way.

I had seen the end of our relationship so many times; we were off and on over three long years. After each breakup, I promised it would be the last. In my heart, I knew that he could never be the man that I married, the man that I would spend my life with, but I wouldn't let go. When I realized it was over, I had spent two and a half years in the madness; my mind and my heart were so confused. I didn't know whether I loved him or whether I had just been captured by his charm, intellect, and money. Maybe it was the endless parties and the intoxicating sex.

Eventually he chose between me and the other woman. She had won a battle that she probably never even knew that she had been fighting. I had been his secret, but I had known everything about her. She lived her fairy tale life with him, never knowing I had done all that I could to prevent her happily ever after.

A punch in the face would have been more comforting than the words "I'm getting married on Thursday." It had been a turbulent three years, filled with passion, lust, joy, anger, and rage. Once again, I was in a state of shock and I have no idea how I got home after such a statement. All I know is that I found myself sitting in my closet, exhausted from the tears. It was *over*! I couldn't believe all the nights that we had laid in my bed and he had shared his life with me. He shared his hopes, his dreams, his fears, and his insecurities; he shared with me that part of himself that others didn't get a chance to witness. The macho bravado got checked at the door with us. I know that he wanted the peace

that he felt with me to just be himself, but he couldn't face the

world with his true identity. He couldn't be sincere or vulnerable

in a world that idolized dominance and testosterone driven

success. I had put up with so much heartache and the dichotomy

of those two worlds had finally torn us apart. I had given my body

to this man in ways that I never even knew I had the talent to

give, and he would marry *her* on Thursday. Maybe all the things

that he had told me about her were lies to keep me around,

knowing that I would never have stayed if I had felt that she was a

threat or that the relationship they had was real.

Early in our relationship, he had quickly explained away

that he was about to become a father. He made it seem as if it

were a business relationship that produced the child. He said it

was an obligation and there was no emotional involvement. He

made me believe that she was just the mother of his child, but I

was "the true love of his life." Maybe he had been telling the

truth, but it didn't matter; he had chosen to marry her and not me.

Eventually, I came to realize that he knew that he could have us both, and I was the one he knew he could manipulate. I had already accepted their relationship at face value. I believed what he had to say, and had continued to see him, in spite of all of my reservations. I ignored my spiritual upbringing, denied the tug at my heart that I felt when I found out that she was having his child, and I made the choice not to walk away.

I stayed and suffered the consequences of my actions. There are those days when things get so bad that you feel like your debts should be paid for with the tears of your suffering; that all the bad things that you've done in your life should be settled with the chaos that exist at the moment. But you really forget all the injustices that you've set into motion and don't know what God is applying to what. That's why I believe I shut down; I was overwhelmed by the burdens of my sins and my guilt, I wondered if I could be forgiven by God, and questioned my ability to forgive myself. I tried to sort out my feelings by writing and late one night

my emotions spilled over to the pages of an empty notebook:

PAY THE PRICE

I KNOW I WAS WRONG
I KNOW YOU WERE RIGHT,
BUT I FELL IN LOVE
BEFORE I COULD FIGHT

THE FEELINGS THAT I FELT
THE PAIN THAT I WAS IN
THE FEELINGS THAT I KNEW
I KNEW WOULD DO ME IN

BUT I FOLLOWED MY EMOTIONS
AND ALLOWED YOU INSIDE
I FOLLOWED MY HEART
AND GAVE LOVE ANOTHER TRY

YOU TOLD ME NOT TO LOVE YOU
THAT WE COULD NEVER BE
YOU TOLD ME NOT TO LOVE YOU
THERE WERE OTHER PRIORITIES

BUT I WAS A FOOL IN LOVE
BLIND TO THE GAME
I WAS A FOOL IN LOVE
AND NOW IT'S TIME TO PAY

NIGHTS SPENT ALONE
WONDERING WHERE I WENT WRONG
NIGHTS SPENT ALONE
TRYING TO GET YOU TO COME HOME

COUNTLESS SLEEPLESS NIGHTS
WONDERING WHY THIS AND WHY THAT

WHAT DID I DO
TO HAVE HIM TREAT ME WITH DISRESPECT

WE'VE ALL BEEN THERE
WE'VE ALL LOVED AND LOST
WE'VE ALL BEEN THERE
WHEN THE BROTHER LAID DOWN THE COST

WE'VE TURNED A DEAF HEAR
AND NOW HE'S THE CASHIER
WE WILL PAY WITH OUR HEART, MIND, BODY & SOUL
WE WILL PAY WITH THE VERY THING WE WILL CLAIM HE STOLE

BUT THE BROTHER WAS TRUE
YET WE CALL HIM A DOG
THE BROTHER WAS TRUE
NOW WE OWE THE COST

COUNT UP THE COST
BEFORE YOU GIVE YOURSELF AWAY
COUNT UP THE COST
OR YOU WILL ALWAYS PAY

Soon after Keilan had announced the whole marriage

thing, and the shock of it had worn off, I began to slowly acclimate

myself back into the humdrum of living my life. I was trying to

accept it, trying to let it go and move on by doing what was right.

For a while, I did pretty well. I resisted calling, until my car broke

down. Keilan was bad for me on so many levels, but he had

provided me with financial support. I still had feelings for him, at least sexually, and I didn't have $1,300 for a new car engine, so I called.

It didn't take much talking on his part, to get back into my bed. When he brought the money over for the car, he apologized for hurting me. He said he didn't want to, but he had to do what was best for the future of his son. There was more, but I had stopped listening after sorry. Unfortunately, that night would drastically alter the rest of our lives.

After a night so typical of many others over the years, he left and I stood in front of my mirror staring at myself; people always told me that I was a pretty girl but, to tell you the truth I didn't see anything. I looked pass myself, not knowing my own image. When I stared into my own eyes, my true self, the person who lives on the inside just seemed lost. That night, I began to unravel.

I had realized that I was that girl begging for another

chance with a man who was walking away. I was that girl whose life seemed to be ending because a man didn't return her phone calls. I was needy and that made me feel dirty. I felt helpless when it came to protecting myself from being hurt and that made me a little mad.

So, I called him to see how he really felt about me; I needed to know that I wasn't just tripping on myself because I felt bad about sleeping with another woman's husband. The phone began to ring and my heart dropped; I was scared to death of what he might say, afraid that he would bluntly admit that he had just been horny and he knew he could have me, but there was no answer. He had just left my apartment five minutes before, so I knew he had heard his phone ring, and I knew that he had caller I.D. So why wasn't he answering?

I called over and over with no answer. I was freaking out, leaving message after message; some sweet, some angry, some sad, some distraught, but no matter what I had to say or how I chose to say it, he had *no answer*!

I began to drive around town, looking for him. I wanted to make him feel what I was feeling, even though I didn't know how I was going to make that happen; I looked anyway. The longer I drove, the more upset I became; thoughts were coming from every direction and each one was more insane than the next.

So, I drove to his home and waited outside in my car. I was on the verge of total breakdown. I was thinking so hard, so quick; flashes of things I wanted to do passed through my mind: bricks through his windows, running him over with my car, sleeping with someone else, fighting her, spray painting his car, pleading with him for an answer to why her and not me.

I couldn't comprehend his actions, couldn't process the thoughts fast enough. Was I the stupidest girl in the world right then? If not, I sure felt like it. I had become so excited that it felt like my heart was pounding outside of my chest. I squeezed my keys so tightly, that I could feel my pulse in the palm of my hand.

Just when I thought my brain would explode, something in me went limp. I stopped, just stopped.

Slowly, I released my keys from the death grip that I had them in, cranked up my vehicle, and drove back to my apartment where the walls seemed colder and the furniture somewhat cheaper than it did just a few hours before. I peeled away my clothing in a state of lethargy, crawled into bed and stared blankly at the walls. I was empty, had nothing else to give, my spirit felt dead, my soul was bare.

I was tripping hard and I knew it, I wasn't productive anymore, my life wasn't moving forward. I was stuck in idle, not going anywhere. I had let a man bring me to the point where I was nothing without him. I questioned my every move and my every thought hinged on his opinion. I'd finally realized that I couldn't continue seeing him, but I had no idea how to move on.

Moving on meant facing that I had crossed the ultimate no-no line; **the *never* say *never* of all time, for me.** I had done the one thing that I detested the most: I'd had an affair with a married man. I had to face my own judgment; *I had to face me*!

"Dealing with me is like dealing with the devil."

His words rang so clearly to me now. Saying I felt stupid for not listening to him was a gross understatement. He had used me and I had let him. For years I had let him, when he told me that he was getting married, when he told me that she would always be a part of his life, and when he told me that I would always be the other woman, I continued to see him. As badly as I wanted to blame Keilan, it wasn't his fault. He had done exactly what he'd told me he would do.

I so badly wanted to believe that the road I chose to travel was the right one and the decisions I had made along the way were justifiable, but who was I kidding? They weren't. I had made so many mistakes; I soon began to question whether or not I knew myself at all.

Alicia Andrews, 5'8", 132lbs, a pretty, chocolate girl by

most people's standards; I was college educated, fun loving, open hearted, and a great dancer. I didn't complain much, I was addicting in the bedroom, I cooked, cleaned and, O.K., I was difficult at times, but nobody's perfect. And in the grand scheme of things what did any of that mean? I didn't know and didn't care; I was lost. I had no energy to try to figure out why I did what I did, so I just laid there, staring blankly at stark white walls that visually represented everything I knew about who I was or what my purpose on earth might be. I was disgusted with the life that was mine. I'd wasted five long years and what did I have to show for it? I had a broken heart, a broken spirit and memories that would keep me forever connected to the most hurtful decisions of my life.

Many years would pass after that first night I took my detour into the abyss of adultery. I don't want to make the path I chose seem like a common mistake that most people make because it's not. Were my feelings valid, yes, but it didn't make any of the acts

I committed right or okay. My decisions to do what made me feel good affected more than just me; the repercussions of my actions would leave a trail of destruction that I would have to account for.

I won't lie and say I faced it right away, because I didn't. I avoided the truth by moving from state-to-state. I built a wall around my heart to protect me from myself. I became ice cold – nothing could penetrate the fortress I had constructed.

But, no matter where I went, Keilan would follow; he had so masterfully alienated me from my friends and family that I felt completely and utterly alone. There was no one I could call, because all of my girlfriends had warned me and pleaded that I leave him alone and I'd never bothered to listen to their advice. My family didn't even know who he was much less anything about the life I had carried on with him. I was terrified to tell them about my lifestyle. I tried to talk to God and even then I felt stupid trying to pray, but I knew that He was my only answer.

CHAPTER 8
FLASHBACK TO REALITY

What in the world? Oh my goodness, how long have I been in this tub? What is going on with me today? I hurriedly got out of the tub and slipped on a strawberry that had dropped out of my hand when I fell asleep, almost an hour before. My vanity chair broke my fall. I felt like I was definitely losing my mind, and apparently my hand and eye coordination as well.

I got dressed and headed to the kitchen. I didn't feel like cooking that night and I wondered what the relatives were doing in the valley, so I called.

"Hello."

"Hey, Roxy, it's Tee." (that's my nickname)

"Hey girl, what's up?"

"Girl, I don't know, I've been tripping all day. I went to the gym earlier and nearly blacked out. I was on the treadmill for about three hours without even realizing it, When I tried to get off, I almost fainted and some guy in there working out got me some water. So, that got me back to the apartment, but then I got in the tub and fell asleep for an hour. After I almost had a heart attack waking up, getting out of the tub, I slipped and fell on a strawberry I had taken in there with me! I'm tripping!"

"You sound like me mailing my bills back to myself the other day, but you don't smoke, so what's your excuse?" she says excitedly.

Laughing out loud, I said, "Girl I don't know, but whatever it is, I wish it would go away, because I ain't got time for this."

"Girl, guess what I did today?"

"Oh, no! What?"

"I had Roscoe put to sleep."

"You did?"

"I had to Tee, I went in the back yard this morning and he just looked at me like, Mommy, I'm tired." So, I put him in the car and took him on down. The doctors examined him and said he was in great health, but his kidneys were going out, because he was so old. Roscoe was seventeen, that's a hundred and something in dog years, you know. I just held him in my arms until he breathed his last breath. That bothered me so bad; I've had Roscoe longer than I've had any of my kids. That was my baby, but I couldn't let him suffer anymore."

"I'm sorry to hear that, but he did live a long life."

"Can't you see I'm on the phone, what do you want that can't wait? I'm talking to Tee." She yelled at the kids in the background.

"Sounds like you have your hands full over there, let me let you go. I have to go return this expensive sweater I bought that can't seem to keep up with its' buttons. These things are falling off for the heck of it and for $400 I'm not sewing them back on. I'm coming out there a little later, do you need anything?"

"No, I'm cool."

"O.K. I'll see you guys in a little while."

My aunt was more like a girlfriend to me. She was, in fact the only girlfriend that I had in Los Angeles. It had been hard to find genuine people in that city, and I was too impatient to start a new search.

I had pursued acting & modeling on the side while I was in Texas and the agency that I was signed to had an office in Los Angeles. Earlier that year we made a trip out to LA for an actors' expo and I did really well. I believed that I could make a life for myself on the West Coast and I needed to get out of San Antonio. So I moved. The only people I knew in the city were my Uncle David and his family. Thank God I got along with his wife and kids. Initially the move to Los Angeles was frustrating, because finding work there was much more difficult than it was back home. My expectations were so high when I first arrived, that when things didn't happen as quickly as I wanted them to, I got very depressed.

I had been away from Florida for nearly five years by this time and I had made some risky decisions in my life. I knew my family had questions about what I was doing. When they called or I called them, the first question would be "how is everything going, you landed anything big yet?" Every time, I felt like a failure when I had to tell them, "not yet," but it's coming. Secretly, I wanted to give it all up. I found no comfort, no spiritual enjoyment, and no happiness in the business itself, at least not in front of the camera. I became disgusted with what I saw going on behind the scenes, as well. I was tired of being judged for my appearance and for how I spoke. It was frustrating to know that even if I got the part, I wouldn't be satisfied. Even if I found fame and riches, it would be insignificant to who I was as a person, on the inside.

I liked looking the part, but I wanted people to look at me and see pretty, but know power. I wanted the first thing people said about me to be "she's intelligent, strong willed, and confident." Then pretty would be the icing on the cake. I couldn't see that happening if I based my success on my ability to look good.

After five years and everyone anticipating that big break that I had talked about so much, I was afraid of what they would say if I redirected my desires. I had borrowed so much money to keep things afloat. I'd put off my education and never really got a 9 to 5, because it would get in the way of my acting and modeling. I knew that my family wanted me to come home or least move a little closer. They felt that I was too far away for them to help me when I needed them the most. I had a car that constantly gave me problems and setting me back financially. My bills were always behind, and I had to borrow money from all over the place to stay afloat. I had lost focus; my hands were in so many different pots that I couldn't remember why I was trying so hard to be in a city that I didn't even like.

I had left San Antonio for the most part to separate myself from Keilan, but even that great a distance didn't deter him from continuing to pursue me. Every summer he flew to LA to attend basketball camp and of course he would always come knocking on my door the second he landed. At first I tried to keep him at bay, but I just didn't have enough integrity to say no to him. LA was an expensive town and work was difficult to come by, so I became to him what I really was anyway. I'm not going to sweeten this up for you guys I was his whore! I use to try and make it sound acceptable, he was my boo, he just takes care of me and I take care of him, I'm his "girlfriend" or better yet, we were friends with benefits. RIIIIIIGGGGGHHHHHTTTT!!! The truth of the matter is for me and for you if this is the lifestyle you choose, is that we can be defined as nothing more than a common whore! It was indeed a tough pill for me to swallow, but I would no longer continue to cover up who I was. I needed to see her – I needed to know her – I had to understand who this girl that I stare at in the mirror

everyday was! We just had to meet!

CHAPTER 9
FLORIDA BOND

I started back attending church while I was in California; it was a foreign atmosphere to me because I had been gone for so long. I'd gone back, looking for answers to my insanity, and even though I was feeling nothing in those services, I kept going back.

I knew that God had to takeover somehow, I didn't know how to make that happen, I just did whatever I could. I didn't research the ministries before I attended, I didn't try to figure out who they were, what their vision or mission was – my life was jacked up and none of that mattered I just needed a message of hope and to be honest with you I was done with the *extra* of church. The fluff and legality of religion was a *no go* for me. I needed God to be real, tangible, I needed His voice to be audible *flat out*! And to keep it

100 with you, if I didn't get that I was deuces, gone!

Everything in my life was falling apart. I cut Keilan off, I lost my job; I was evicted from my apartment and I had nowhere to go, but home. I really believed that moving to California from Texas would help me, but I was wrong, I knew deep down that Florida would be the only place he would not follow, so home is where I was headed.

I still had my little Mitsubishi Eclipse, and an apartment filled with furniture and appliances that I couldn't take with me. I had every intention of going back to Panama City, getting a summer waitress job to make some quick money, and heading back to my life in Cali — so I rented a storage unit, packed away my things, said my goodbyes to my California family and prepared for the long ride home.

I was an empty mess and the drive from across the country was an uneventful journey. The trees blurred by as the scenery merged into nothingness. My mind was consumed with the mistakes I'd made. What explanation could I give my family and friends for the life I'd been living?

I returned home to start a new life or something that resembled what my life was to become. The old church family welcomed me in, and I began another journey down a new road...to a new place!

I did my best to erase the memory of the life I had created with Keilan, but that would be impossible. He would forever be a part of my life now, as the father of my child. My daughter is the only bright light that shines from that dark period.

Oh yeah, I kind of left that part out. I was devastated to find out that I was pregnant with his child and to be honest abortion weighed heavily on my mind. I so wanted a clean break from him, but that would not be my path. God had a plan for me that included Keilan, a plan that included her, my sweet child. I was so bitter when I returned to my home state and my anger grew over time and if it had not been for my child I would have not recovered. On the bad days when I was depressed and sad, beating myself up over the things that I had done, she would out the blue come up to me and give me the sweetest hugs and say, "mommy I love you," and just a glimmer of hope would rise in me.

I couldn't allow my anger towards Keilan tarnish who she would become, so I had to forgive him and ultimately I had to forgive myself.

Years after our relationship ended, I felt that I still owed his wife an apology. I had moved on and Keilan and I were able to deal with one another pretty civilly. I had re-established a relationship with Christ. I was in a completely surrendered life unto God. So, the fact that she didn't know bothered me, I just didn't feel as though I would be able to move forward in what I know that God was calling forth for me to do with the weight of what I had done to her on my shoulders. Mind you, she never knew about me, so my daughter was of course a secret as well. I felt stupid, scared, and ashamed of what I had to tell her, but I couldn't go on with my life as if I had done nothing. I warned

Keilan that I would be doing it and he was indifferent at that point because unannounced to me she had just found out and he had already dealt with the heaviness of the issue and it was not so good for him. We had never met face-to-face, but I knew who she was, so I found her on Facebook and sent her an apology via message. I explained who I was and expressed my sincere apology for any pain or disrespect that my actions may have caused her.

My daughter was seven years old by then. I had gotten married, had another daughter, and a third one was on the way. I had forgiven myself; God had forgiven me. I had even forgiven Keilan, but I still held onto guilt about her.

She had discovered the true nature of our relationship through child support papers. He had never told her and I didn't feel like it was my place, so I left it up to him. I wanted Keilan to be happy with her and their kids, and I needed her to know that I accepted my role in the affair and I would never be a threat to her household.

She thanked me for being honest, but asked that, out of respect, I not contact her again. I agreed and that was it! I was free and hopefully, so was she! I couldn't judge their relationship. I didn't understand it from my viewpoint, but it wasn't for me to understand. She had her reasons for staying with him and I had to respect that.

I wish I had a fairy tale ending for this story, wish that I could paint a pretty picture of how it all turned out for me, but I can't. Because, even as I place pen to paper, I am in the midst of my new hopes, my joys, my daily pains, my past, and my future. I am closer than I was even a day ago. I have chosen to love the person that I am. I now know the real Alicia, the person that Jehovah designed and purposed me to be. I am a child of the most High King. I was created with intent to effect change on this Earth and in others that I encounter. My past is not pretty. I have done things that I am not at all proud of. I am embarrassed to admit I actually did some of these things that I did and what I have shared here is only a piece of the puzzle that completes me.

However, this girl, AliWatts, knows that she is forgiven. I am following my heart down a path that feels right in every respect. I am still in the process of cultivating my relationship with my God and a never-ending battle with my enemy, both in spirit and flesh. I still love, cry, complain, hope and pray that one day that I will "get it right," whatever that means. Life is complicated only because we make it that way, but I'm convinced that it can be simple.

I now know that my freedom is in the knowledge of the Father and His Kingdom. My freedom is in fully understanding why I am here on earth and knowing that my life is lived for a purpose greater than me. I don't know why it was so hard for me to get to that point of knowing why I chose to travel the path that I did to get here, but I am grateful that He didn't leave me in the middle of my mess. I am so grateful that my friends and family didn't give up on me. I am grateful that there are still people, yes people, in the body of Christ that love Him for real and don't judge me by my past. They see me for the potential that lies within. I am a Kingdom citizen and I walk within the rights that I possess as such. Now I hold fast to the teachings of the Holy Bible where in the book of Proverbs 3:5 & 6 states:

Trust in the Lord with all thine heart; and lean not unto thine own understanding. In all of thy ways acknowledge him, and he shall direct thy path.

That scripture is etched in my heart and I will rely on its promise forever. Life is what it is! I've said it before and I'll say it again,

"Even if you try to sugarcoat it for others, no matter how hard you try, you can't sugarcoat it for yourself."

I have to believe that the path that I choose now, and choose each day, is the right one. Sometimes, I still wonder if I've made a few wrong turns when presented with multiple options. But there is always this stirring in my inner spirit, a place that I can't reach physically, but I know is there, that lets me know the path that I'm on is mine. It was my choice to walk it, and the destination and consequences are mine to deal with; and deal with them I shall. I'm a person that presents both positive and negative traits; I love whole-heartedly, always have and always will. I accepted the Lord as my personal Savior long ago and strayed from the faith. But I'm home again and I am in a place of peace, a place of acceptance, a place of love. Regardless of what others may think, I take the commitment I have made to my Lord seriously. I've made my mistakes and I'm positive that before it's all over, I'll make more. Not because I know I will be forgiven, but because I'm human and we do that. No matter what, I'll die knowing that I'm doing what Holy Spirit guides me to do and living my life according to the knowledge of His Word that I possess and whatever my reward or punishment, I gladly receive it, with no preconceived expectations!

CHAPTER 10
DON'T BE A REPEAT OFFENDER

My name is every name, I am every girl, every woman, every boy, and every man who as ever loved and lost, only to repeat the mistakes that made him or her lose love in the first place. The lesson never seems to be learned, the behaviors never seem to be changed. The people may be different, but the relationships are the same.

I am a firm believer that we seek what is comfortable and attract what we expect for ourselves. Until we expect more, we will never have what our hearts desire – true love, unconditional acceptance, and perfect peace with people who we can just be ourselves with completely; no pretending, no holding back, just being you — bare and naked before another person — being completely real without reservation.

I never really considered myself a Maury Povich, Jerry Springer, Reality TV drama-queen type, but the proof is in the pudding. Talk is cheap and actions are worth their weight in gold. If you and I would take a true look over our lives, most of us would have to admit that we've been the person who always went back to the cheater, even when faced with the truth. We've been the person on the side who knew they would never leave their spouse. We've been the one who craved attention at any cost, regardless of the embarrassment that would follow us for the rest of our days. We were the ones most people never would have guessed had a past as colorful as ours was. I was the girl who wanted *your* approval; yes *you,* the person reading this book. Even though we've never met, I felt like I needed you to say I was okay, I was good; I was worthy. And even though I want it, I no longer need anybody's approval to move forward, to *do me,* and my love, neither do you!

ABOUT THE AUTHOR

Hello world, this is your girl, AliWatts. I am a goofy girl at heart and I have a passion for life, liberty, and the pursuit of all that God has for me!

I have embraced my uniqueness, my mistakes, my triumphs, and my destiny in life. I understand my place in the world and now I am most passionate about seeing that same passion released in others.

I am the owner, alongside my husband, of Global Vocal Entertainment, a full service production and promotions company, where I operate as a communication specialist that focuses on visual stimulus through the written word, spoken/lyrical voice and video production. I am a graduate of Florida State University with a B.A. in Communication and I am the Director of Public Relations and Media at Kingdom Agenda International Ministry, in Panama City, Florida.

I believe that we design our world with what's on the inside of us and how we release it determines the impact it will have on others.

I challenge you to Live Your Passion wholeheartedly and with no regret move forward into your destined place in God!

Connect with Me Socially
FACEBOOK: AliWatts
TWITTER: @wattsalicia
INSTAGRAM: wattsali
www.aliciawatts.com
www.globalvocalent.com

www.ingramcontent.com/pod-product-compliance
Lightning Source LLC
LaVergne TN
LVHW051514080426
835509LV00017B/2064